"...Do you feel like you have a brick sitting in your gut? Did you recently eat a heap of tater tots? A bowl of pasta? Deep-dish pizza? Well, you will always be jealous of friends/mates who skip to the loo if you keep eating like that. Heed *The Un-Constipated Gourmet!*"

—Dr. Louis Stule, author of *Don't Wait to Go**

"A must-have for pregnant women, couch potatoes, brooders, world travelers, Northern Europeans, and everyone over 40 who loves to eat gourmet food... and can't get it out..."

—Constance Pater, President, Colonoscopy Society*

"...the *Freakonomics* of food...a rogue chef explores the *other* side of everything edible."

—Stu K. Cooke, editor of *Occupado* magazine*

"This book is nothing short of a public service..."

—Association of W.C. Attendants*

D1412610

*These people don't exist—to the author's knowledge—but they speak the truth.

The
UN·CONSTIPATED
GOURMET

Secrets to a Moveable Feast

Danielle Svetcov

 SOURCEBOOKS, INC.®
NAPERVILLE, ILLINOIS

Published by Sourcebooks, Inc.
P.O. Box 4410, Naperville, Illinois 60567-4410
(630) 961-3900
Fax: (630) 961-2168
www.sourcebooks.com

Library of Congress Cataloging-in-Publication Data

Svetcov, Danielle.
    The un-constipated gourmet : secrets to a moveable feast : 125 recipes for the
regularity challenged / Danielle Svetcov.
        p. cm.
    Includes bibliographical references and index.
    1. Constipation--Diet therapy--Recipes. I. Title.
    RC861.S84 2009
    641.5'631--dc22
                            2009003138

Printed and bound in the United States of America
CHG 10 9 8 7 6 5 4 3 2

To family, alive and in heaven, who gave me guts.

Contents

"…bran? You might as well eat rope and yank it through."

—Nedda, from the play Frankie & Johnny in the Clair de Lune

"Like many people, my parents believed that a 'normal' digestive tract must cleanse itself of waste every day. They insisted that I was born constipated."

—Jane E. Brody, "Looking Beyond Fiber to Stay 'Regular,'" New York Times,
August 2, 2005 (the most-read article of that day)

"Even my best stuff ends up as crap."

—someone told me that Mario Batali once said this, but I can't find a reference to it anywhere.
I hope he said it, because it's true…of everybody's best stuff

A Few Preliminary Words on Fiber

by *Anish A. Sheth, MD, gastroenterologist and Assistant Professor of Medicine at Yale University School of Medicine*

One needn't look any further than the recalcitrant kernels of corn embedded in our stool to realize that what comes out is determined in large part by what goes in. And while it seems impossible at times to keep up with the perpetually changing list of "superfoods," the prescription for healthy bowels is refreshingly simple—fiber, fiber, and more fiber. Yup, we're talking good ol' fashioned roughage. Lost amidst the açaí shakes and bee-pollen supplements is the simple truth that a diet high in fiber yields not only long-sought-after regularity but countless other health benefits as well. And while few would discount the physical and emotional upside of regular, effortless (yes, even enjoyable) bowel movements, until now eating fiber has been equated with gritty glasses of Metamucil and intolerable bran cereal. But fear fiber no more—The Un-Constipated Gourmet's collection of recipes promises to make consumption of high-fiber foods every bit as pleasurable as their eventual egress.

Before diving into the nitty-gritty of how fiber works its magic, one must take a moment to appreciate the irony of this astonishing substance. Our intestines have evolved over millions of years to be able to digest virtually everything we eat—the toughest T-bone steak and most decadent chocolate cheesecake are no match for our digestive juices. So how is it, then, that a measly kernel of corn can travel through 25 feet of intestine and resist the effects of acid, bile, and digestive enzymes? Even more remarkable is that a substance that emerges unchanged in our stool can play such a vital role in the health of our GI tract. Pile on fiber's ability to decrease the risk of developing colon cancer and one can't help but develop a healthy obsession with all things fibrous.

The story of fiber begins with the foods we eat. Fiber is a naturally occurring substance presumably put on Earth to keep its inhabitants happy and regular. All fiber, however, is not created equal. Soluble fiber and insoluble fiber are the terms given to the two main classes of this wondrous substance. A third, lesser known but equally important member of the fiber family is known as resistant starch.

The main difference between the two main types of dietary fiber (soluble and insoluble) lies in their divergent fates once inside the human body. Insoluble fiber, found in foods like wheat bran and, yes, corn on the cob (Elote, page 123), travels through the GI tract without being altered and comes out looking much like it did on the way in. Insoluble fiber's main benefit is to add bulk to stools and thereby prevent constipation.

Foods high in soluble fiber, such as legumes and nuts (Nut Shake, page 18), on the other hand, are processed not by our intestines, but by bacteria living in our gastrointestinal tract. Our colons are loaded with trillions of bacteria whose main function is to turn the fiber we eat into byproducts that our body can use. Among these products is a gel-like substance that lubricates the colon's inner lining. This magical gel not only keeps stools pillowy soft and allows for a frictionless journey down the intestinal tract, but it also nurtures the colonic cells, potentially accounting for fiber's benefit with regard to prevention of colon cancer. And just to show that there is truly no such thing as a free lunch (especially if it's one high in fiber), the process of bacterial fermentation causes production of a most undesirable derivative, methane gas.

Resistant starch is a third form of fiber that combines the health benefits of soluble and insoluble types of fiber. So named because of its ability to escape digestion in the small intestine, resistant starch travels to the colon, where it helps stimulate growth of healthy bacteria and contributes to overall colonic health. Foods high in resistant starch include such varied provisions as bananas (the greener the better), navy beans, and cold potatoes.

So what are the honest-to-goodness health benefits of a high-fiber diet? The answer to this question comes from comparing rates of diseases between parts of the world that eat a lot of fiber (e.g., Asia) to those that don't (e.g., North America, northern Europe). What we find is that eating fiber seems to protect you from a host of GI diseases ranging from hemorrhoids to diverticulosis (small pockets in the colon that can bleed or become inflamed) to dreaded colon cancer. Throw in benefits to cholesterol levels and prevention of heart disease, and it seems clear that fiber is a superfood in its own right.

The most noticeable (and some would argue, the most important) benefit of fiber is its ability to make once-dreaded trips to the toilet enjoyable again. Let's face it, constipation is no fun. Fiber has the ability to turn stooling sessions previously full of grunting and perspiration into blissful and wonderfully effortless experiences. Mocking poo pebbles in the toilet bowl are replaced with the coveted single, large, S-shaped coil. Who knows? With a lot of fiber and a little luck, you may one day experience poo-phoria, the post-evacuation feeling of rapturous relaxation, considered by experts to be the pinnacle of poo performance.

(For those of you not expecting to read vivid descriptions of fiber-enriched poo, my apologies. This is a cookbook, after all.)

With all these benefits, it's a wonder that the average American only manages to scarf down a third of the recommended 25 to 35 grams of fiber a day. That's right. For all the whole-grain breads and high-fiber cereals, most of us stumble just to get to the 10 gram/day mark. But who can blame us? After all, most bran cereals taste like freeze-dried cardboard. And prunes? Sure, they taste good, but you would have to toss back a couple dozen to get enough daily fiber. And man cannot survive on prunes alone…

This is where *The Un-Constipated Gourmet* comes in—a cookbook which puts the fun back in fiber. Going far beyond salads (I'll have the gorgonzola and fig, thank you), *The Un-Constipated Gourmet* combines the best fiber-full recipes from around the world, allowing the reader to eat heartily while staying healthy. So go ahead, throw away the tub of Metamucil and toss the bran cereal (but hold onto the prunes—see Tzimmes, page 121), *The Un-Constipated Gourmet* is the only high-fiber product you'll need in your kitchen.

Finally…a cookbook sure to provide regularity in a world of uncertainty, recipes sure to keep America's mouths—and colons—open.

The Registered Dietician Who's Heard It All

Frances Largeman-Roth, RD, Senior Food and Nutrition Editor, Health Magazine

The calls usually start out something like this: "So, Frances, can I ask you a question?" This is usually followed by a series of descriptions of visits (or nonvisits) to the bathroom, with my friend adding in the occasional, "I hope I'm not grossing you out." Of course they're not, because I've heard it all.

As a registered dietician and the Senior Food and Nutrition Editor of Health magazine, I've been privy to the digestive complaints of many people for the past ten years. Nearly every girlfriend of mine has had some kind of GI issue, and a handful even had to have invasive tests done before their thirtieth birthdays. It seems that stomach problems—including abdominal pain, bloating, and constipation—are indeed one of the most prevalent medical complaints, creating countless days of missed work each year. One reason for all these problems may be a lack of fiber. Most Americans only get 10 to 15 grams of fiber each day, but health groups advise getting between 25 to 35 grams a day.

Along with all those slightly panicked calls from friends ("Frances, it's been days since I've gone!"), I've also seen lots of products and remedies promising relief from constipation and other GI symptoms. Fiber-filled cookies, bars, shakes, and muffins have all had their moment in the sun. Some might be helpful, but others (often those packed with psyllium hulls and chicory fiber) just tend to produce more gas in your gut, making you even more uncomfortable than you already were.

As with nutrients like calcium and iron, the best way to get enough fiber is to eat foods that are naturally rich in it on a daily basis. That way, you're getting an entire nutrient package in a great-tasting food, not fiber that's built into a crumbly bar or hay-like drink. That's why I love Danielle's approach—just eat tasty, healthy foods that get you going naturally. And guess what? Eating all these foods that are naturally rich in fiber will help lower your cholesterol and prevent diseases like diverticulitis and possibly even colon cancer. Plus, you're likely to drop a few pounds because you'll feel more full.

When Danielle first told me about her idea for The Un-Constipated Gourmet, I thought it was brilliant. No one has really approached the topic of uh...pooping with so much wit and honesty, and certainly not with so much taste. Danielle tackles an issue that nearly everyone will face at some point in life, whether it's due to stress, dehydration, change in diet, travel, pregnancy, injury, or advancing age. And unlike so much advice on the market these day, this book doesn't ask you to do anything crazy, like eliminate whole food groups, or buy far-flung ingredients, or excavate your colon to get the benefits of good digestion.

So the next time you're backed up, don't wait around for things to work themselves out, or drink gallons of prune juice or packets of Metamucil—just flip to page 115 for a yummy helping of Chard with Miso and Sesame. Of course, don't forget to wash it down with a tall glass of water.

Introduction

Most gourmets value the sublime flavor of the food they prepare and eat. And the texture. The temperature. The exotic origins. The presentation. I'm a gourmet, and I appreciate those things too. But, in the back of my mind, I'm thinking about one additional, all-important criterion: will this lead me, eventually, to the john?

I am not the only one with this preoccupation. We're a population divided into haves and have-nots. Have used the facilities today and have not. The haves know who they are. They can eat nothing but potatoes and biscuits for a week and still whistle en route to the potty. The have-nots are a more downbeat crowd. They take up smoking. They tap their feet at meetings. They spend time lurking near bathrooms, mouthing silent prayers, but never actually entering. We are the butt of jokes, literally.

If you look at recent stats, we are actually a very large group:

1. Number of visits to office-based physicians for digestive system symptoms in 2004: 41.3 million (Source: National Ambulatory Medical Care Survey)

2. Number of yearly doctor visits in the U.S. due to constipation: at least 2.5 million (Source: The American College of Gastroenterology)

3. Average number of work days missed by a person suffering from gastrointestinal disorders in the U.S.: 1 per week, in a 40-hour workweek (Source: Annual Scientific Meeting of the American College of Gastroenterology)

4. Diverticulosis alone—the disease that doctors claim is a direct result of constipation and a low-fiber diet—affects one out of every two people over the age of 60. (Source: National Digestive Diseases Information Clearinghouse)

5. Age the author had her first colonoscopy: 21.

Still, despite our numbers, this inability to "go" is mostly a private preoccupation. We buy Weetabix and Metamucil in bulk and quietly and shamefully pray that the checkout lady will think it's for the kids. But this silent suffering is fairly new. "The amount of attention that both medical and lay writers have lavished on the costive bowel over the last centuries is enormous..." according to James C. Whorton in his magnificently scatological tome, *Inner Hygiene: Constipation and the Pursuit of Health in Modern Society* (Oxford, 2000). Whorton reveals a time between 1800 and 1950 when defecation was the *American Idol* of bodily functions. "No single harmful effect of civilization was warned about more frequently than constipation." Treatises on the subject sold in the tens of thousands. You couldn't turn a corner without bumping into an advertisement for purgatives (Jam-o-Lax, Lax-Krax, Purgo, Purgil, Purgatin, Purglets). Advertorial booklets "itemized and explained the ravages of intestinal stasis." One such booklet was called "The Story of Constipation"—as if the whole family might gather around with hot cocoa and enjoy.

Frankly, I'm glad we've toned ourselves down. That it's now an affliction—mumbled about under one's breath or to one's uncorked, gloating spouse—seems much more appropriate. We've rendered the subject innocuous with words like "roughage" and "fiber." We do not have to see our sorry selves portrayed on billboards or television, and really, except for the occasional mound in the street left by a dog and the inordinate attention paid to diapers, popular discourse is nearly free of poop today.

Still, whether shouted from rooftops or mumbled amidst expletives, the obsession persists. And what truly astounds is that after all this time, we've yet to solve the problem in any satisfying way. And by satisfying, I mean gourmet.

So, consummate fixer that I am, last year I began quietly amassing a recipe collection—delicious dishes from around the world that have the double benefit of tasting great and calling you to duty. I'm not talking about mixing Metamucil into risotto, or spiking the Brandy Manhattan with prune juice. I'm talking about a recipe collection that stands beside (or perhaps just behind) How to Cook Everything and The Joy of Cooking, that competes on all levels—ease, taste, quality of ingredients, etc.—with great cookbooks for home chefs everywhere.

The collection began with a query to friends and relatives. "I'm working on a little research project and wonder if you can help. It involves food…and, well, the passage of food. Is there a meal or food that's eaten in your home that you rely on to get your bowels moving? Was the recipe passed down to you from ancestors? Is it regional or international in origin? Does it really work or do you think it's all superstition and lore?"

An amazing amount of email arrived in my inbox shortly after. Answers often began with "Pssst, keep my name out of this, but have you ever tried…" They also came with a ridiculous number of exclamation marks. "Oh my God!!!!!!!! This is so great!!!!!! My family is obsessed with this topic!!!!!"

Once I'd collected two dozen recipes, I began more formal research. I wanted to know if what I'd been handed had any validity when held up against science and history. In the process, I turned up some fantastic resources, which I allude to in the pages that follow. Among them: *The Natural Laxative Cookbook, Inner Hygiene: Constipation and the Pursuit of Health in Modern Society,* and *Life Is Like a Chicken Coop Ladder.*

Along the way, I also discovered that there really isn't anything quite like *The Un-Constipated Gourmet.* Instead, there's a growing unfunny collection of clinical/medical books on the subject (e.g., the *Colon Health Handbook*) and cookbooks (e.g., *The Fiber for Life Cookbook*), none of which I can imagine gripping to my chest while giddily dancing around my kitchen.

If it's not already obvious, *The Un-Constipated Gourmet* will not be one of those harpy tomes that tell you to get off your *ass,* exercise, and eat low-fat, flavorless food. I've got no interest in cramping your lifestyle. If you're 50, stare at a computer all day, and then stare at a TV all night, more power to you. Just make time to cook, is all I ask. If you're young and active and still suffer from bathroom envy, then you need this book even more than the couch potatoes.

In fact, there are only three absolute rules for readers:

1. Throw away the laxatives.

2. Cook real food (if it includes an ingredient you can't pronounce or spell phonetically, it's not food).

3. Eat slower, and chew more. (This is age-old wisdom. Platina, the first papal librarian, circa 1470, covered health and diet extensively in his writing. From *Platina: On Right Pleasure and Good Health:* "We might, however, all take warning in one matter: not to swallow food which has not been chewed enough, as many do in our eagerness to eat, for then the stomach works too hard in digestion…")

Everything else in here is optional…though highly recommended.

HOW TO USE THIS BOOK

Now, brass tacks…It's Sunday afternoon and you're ready to grocery shop for the upcoming week. But first, you must plan the meals. You know what you're good at cooking, you know what tastes good, but starting today, you have a new mandate: "Keep my gastrointestinally-challenged family moving…" That's a big challenge.

From here on out, you have a book you can consult before you dive into menu planning. It's your new linchpin. Without it, you won't know the perfect fiber-rich side dish to pair with the guaranteed-to-put-a-cork-in-you pasta carbonara. Without it, you won't know that it's perfectly fine to serve constipating mashed potatoes for dinner, so long as you're having cabbage with miso as a starter and rhubarb sauce on your dessert. In short, by combing through *The Un-Constipated Gourmet* each week and picking recipes from it, the family meal planner knows he or she is going to have a moveable feast.

At the heart of every recipe are ingredients from God's most "effective" food groups (think of them as "Superfoods" with an agenda). Among them are fruits, beans, chocolate, and coffee. Throughout the book, you will learn about their attributes, their histories, and even the lore surrounding them. The complete list, available in the pages that follow, is not without controversy, and I know I will receive a lot of mail from readers with ideas about what should qualify for top billing and what should not. (Please don't write in and tell me cigarettes are God's *real* gift to the gut. Yes, it's true, everything moves smoother with nicotine. But what's the point if you fall off the john from a heart attack?)

Courting further debate, we've ranked each recipe on our Go-Meter (five being the lowest fiber rank on this scale and ten the highest). When eating a "ten," we recommend close proximity to a restroom.

The book is organized by meal type, making it easy for a cook to shuffle through in search of that perfect breakfast, snack, soup, salad, entree, or dessert. And we've got a special chapter called Emergency Recipes (page 217) for those occasions when long-term planning simply didn't pan out and you need a remedy—NOW.

Of special note, in case you're wondering, you will not find trendy new-age food accessories here—sprouts, wheatgrass, groats, kombucha, teff, etc. They may have loads of gut-friendly fiber, or a magical digestive enzyme, but, like tree bark or carob, they simply make gourmet ends difficult to achieve. By that I mean they taste crummy to me. Instead, I made it a priority to script recipes for the discerning palate. Fans of the Food Network and readers of *Saveur* will not be disappointed. Be it dinner-party fare, roll-out-of-bed-and-make-it-with-your-eyes-closed fare, or even emergency fare—it will meet the gourmet standard. (If it makes new-agey foodies feel better, you won't see a lot of white flour, pasta, potatoes, or white rice here either. Not until the Corkage chapter, anyway.)

By the time you're done exploring *The Un-Constipated Gourmet*, you will, I believe, have a new outlook on life, or at least a new outlook on your grocery list. You'll also be able to pick up a menu at Chez Panisse, Bouley, or even the Waffle House, and titter at the offerings. Chard with fish cheeks? Black bean hash. Ha! You'll be able to look behind each food and know its true utility. If all goes well, owners of *The Un-Constipated Gourmet* will be marching to the loo, chins up (leaving the book just outside, please).

KEY FOODS

Gastroenterologists are like trendy restaurants. You get to a certain age, and suddenly friends are asking if you've been yet, what you ordered, and how much it cost. Then, unbidden, they exclaim, "Oh, Dr. Poke-and-prod saved me from myself"—or—"She understood *exactly* what I was going through." That's how I heard about Dr. Bart Kummer, a highly regarded New York City gastroenterologist with twenty-five years of experience. (He happens to be the brother of Corby Kummer, food writer for the *Atlantic Monthly*...brothers on opposite sides of the food chain...I find that amusing.) The day I spoke to Dr. Kummer, he had just finished stretching a patient's esophagus, a procedure I didn't even know was possible. When the good doctor isn't wielding an endoscope, he's speaking to hundreds of patients with gastrointestinal issues, most of them dealing with the common cold of the gastro system—constipation. These patients think they've got a serious problem that will require potent medication. They soon discover that their $20 co-pay has earned them a friendly pamphlet about diet. "Honestly, if people just knew how to eat...Eight out of ten times, the problem is diet," Kummer says.

Which brings us to the subject of **Key Foods**—the stuff you must be eating every day to keep you on the rails.

In almost every case, the key foods in the list below are rich in fiber. Why does fiber make a food more healthy for the gut? Because we humans lack the ability to digest it, so it tears through our systems to get the heck out, dragging all the stuff in the gut with it. (That's an abridged description. For a more scientific assessment, read the comments from Anish Sheth, MD, on pages xi-xiv). For years, doctors told us the best way to get fiber was to sprinkle bran on our breakfast cereals and yogurts. Those of us who were listening complied. What we discovered: Bran is mighty effective. It tears through the gut with so much force that some of us are left dehydrated and crampy after it's made its way through. Not exactly the result we were looking for. In time, some of us figured out that bran is a nice shortcut in an emergency, but because it has the habit of dehydrating eaters, a preferable setup is a daily menu in which fiber shows up in a variety of sources—fruits to beans. Correction—a variety of flavorful sources. That is the aim of this book.

Some people claim that fiber isn't the only way to get the gut moving. In my interviews and research, I stumbled upon plenty of people who believe that hot water, yogurt, eggs, tea, coffee, chocolate, alcohol, cheese, olive oil, and other nonfibrous foods are their best aids. There is little scientific evidence to back these claims, but when you hear a refrain enough times, you start to wonder if there might be some truth to it, and since this book is meant to crack open a topic left dormant for too long, I feel it's my duty to share all my findings and let you determine the efficacy for yourself. Here's that **Key Foods** list:

Hot water	Lentils	Pears
Coffee	Sesame seeds	Apricots
Tea	Pumpkin seeds	Apples
Booze	Flax seeds	Raspberries
Chocolate	Squash	Blackberries
Olive oil	Beets	Mangos
Eggs	Broccoli	Papayas
Miso	Cabbage/Sauerkraut	Cranberries
Cultured yogurt	Chard	Boysenberries
Cheese	Artichokes	Persimmons
Black beans	Brussels Sprouts	Millet
Cannellini beans	Peas	Rice bran
Navy beans	Corn	Oat bran
Chickpeas	Sweet potato	Wheat bran
Lima beans	Rhubarb	Cornmeal
Edamame	Prunes	Bulgur
Cashews	Figs	Barley
Almonds	Dates	
Peanuts	Raisins	

* Many will note the absence of extensive talk about herbs and spices in this book. They comprise such a controversial and lengthy discussion that I thought I ought to shelve them for another day and concentrate on the bulkier portion of the daily diet. But, a basic rule of thumb: the spicier the sauce, the swifter the kick in the pants.

** Except in the Corkage chapter, which I include to help those who overdo their constipation relief, you will see very little white flour, white potato, or pasta here. Why? They represent a trifecta of bad news for those with sluggish digestive systems.

THE TEN PLAGUES OF THE GUT

For some folks, it's not enough to say "eat this and you will feel better." For this mulish bunch, you must also include a "don't-eat-this" list. If you fit this description, then this list is for you. They are all foods with negligent amounts of fiber, which are typically eaten in copious amounts. And if you are prone to stuck guts, they will almost certainly cause you trouble. Imagine a snake swallowing a boulder, and you get the idea.

Bagels

White potatoes

Baguettes

Pancakes

White rice

Pizza

Semolina pasta

Rice noodles

White flour biscuits

Doughnuts

*Of course, there are whole-grain and multigrain versions of most of these, which means more fiber and less gut trouble for the eater; but, as a gourmet, I have a hard time recommending such whole-grain adaptations. The problem with healthy, fiber-rich tweaks to baked goods is they are typically dull and flavorless substitutes for the real thing. Worse, they rarely satisfy your cravings. My recommendation: save these "hazardous" foods for special occasions and take precautions when you do eat them (like eating a bowl of granola on either side of a pizza-pasta-potato feast).

THE GO-METER

You may notice a little icon in the corner of each page where a recipe appears. It resembles a paper scroll of the water-closet variety. This is the symbol for the Go-Meter. Here's a sample under magnification so you know what to look for:

On the scroll, a number between 5 and 10 appears. Five indicates general, reliable efficacy. Ten indicates the most powerful kind of urge. No recipe in this book scores below a 5 on the Go-Meter.

"Of all corporeal operations, digestion has the most powerful influence over the moral state of the individual. Nor ought anyone to be surprised by this assertion; for, indeed, it could not possibly be otherwise…And so our accustomed manner of digesting, with particular reference to the latter part of the process, makes us habitually gay or sad, silent or talkative, morose or melancholy, without our being aware of it, and most certainly without our being able to avoid it."

Jean-Anthelme Brillat-Savarin, The Physiology of Taste, or, Meditations on Transcendental Gastronomy, 1825

"It is impossible to give many of the numerous treatments in so short a space, suffice it to say that the general character of our diet and experience is such as to assure us that at least one-quarter of the food that we swallow is intended by nature to be evacuated from the system; and if it is not, it is again absorbed into the system, poisoning the blood and producing much suffering and permanent disease. The evacuation of the bowels *daily*, and above all, *regularly*, is therefore all important to aid this form of disorder."

Hugo Ziemann, *Steward of the White House, and Mrs. F.L. Gillette*, The White House Cook Book, A Comprehensive Cyclopedia of Information for the Home Containing Cooking, Toilet and Household Recipes, Menus, Dinner-Giving, Table Etiquette, Care of the Sick, Health Suggestions, Facts Worth Knowing, etc., 1905

breakfast

For those who are costive, who eat too many dried and hot meats and have slow guts, the famous English doctor, Humphrey Brooke, recommended roast apples, stewed prunes a half-hour before dinner, and a good "draft" (beer) in the morning.

Hygiene, 1650

galette

1 egg

1½ tablespoons fromage blanc or yogurt

1 tablespoon oat bran

1 tablespoon wheat bran

Pinch of salt (and pepper, if you're serving with savory foods)

Contrary to everything you've heard, the French actually do take measures to watch their weight and maintain healthy eating habits. Point of fact, this galette is popular among France's postpartum women, whose systems, like ours, are a bit run down after childbirth. I know it doesn't sound like much when you read the ingredients, but don't be fooled. They're delicious. Miracle food? Perhaps. Certainly an antidote to the French fry.

MAKES ABOUT THREE SMALL PANCAKES (ENOUGH FOR ONE PERSON)

Mix all ingredients. Let sit for 30 minutes. Fry, in butter or oil, over medium heat in a sauté pan, as 1 large pancake or several small ones. Top with fresh fruit, compote, or syrup. Or serve with savory sautéed greens, like chard or spinach.

Do not eat more than four a day or, I've been warned, you may cramp up. If you prefer a classic pancake-y texture, try adding extra yogurt or fromage blanc in the next batch.

GRAIN BREAKDOWN

A grain is composed of three parts: the germ (the fertile part), the bran (the outer shell), and the starchy reserve used as fuel for the growing seed. The human digestive apparatus can't break down the bran fiber. Instead, the bran serves as "roughage," absorbing water and laying the rebar foundations for a successful b.m. Fiber also gives the digestive muscles something to push against, keeping them toned and taut. While intestinal muscle tone may not win you a hot date, it will keep your innards happy and cleaned out.

WHEAT BRAN

Almost two centuries ago, Sylvester Graham recognized that refined flour was very bad for the intestines. He mixed his nutritional insight with a little religious fervor and widely promoted bread made of whole, or "Graham" flour. Not only did it move your bowels, but it purged your mind of impure thoughts as well. That's what he promised his minions, anyway. Of the various brans available, wheat is perhaps the most harsh, purging the guts rapidly and sometimes causing cramps and dehydration. Coarse wheat bran has a greater effect than finely-ground bran, as its sheer bulkiness stimulates the intestines. Make sure your bran hasn't been cut with sawdust, as was common practice for unscrupulous merchants taking advantage of the Graham fad back in the 1830s.

enlightened bran muffins with sweet potato and cranberries

Most of the bran muffins I know suffer from low self-esteem. They're so worried about being "good" that they forgo tasting good. It is possible to make a bran muffin that's not dry, heavy, and gravelly in the mouth. It just takes a little magic. Here it is.

MAKES A DOZEN

Preheat oven to 400°F. Combine the sweet potato (or pumpkin), wheat bran, eggs, buttermilk, molasses, and sugar in large bowl. Stir with a whisk until smooth. In a separate bowl, mix the flour, baking powder, baking soda, cinnamon, and ginger. Stir the wet ingredients into the dry until moistened. Add the cranberries and pumpkin seeds. Butter two 6-cup muffin tins (you can use paper liners, but you'll miss out on a buttery finish); fill two-thirds full. Bake until tops are brown and spring back when touched, about 25 minutes. Let tins cool on a rack for 10 minutes before removing the muffins. Once cool, refrigerate or freeze.

1 cup mashed cooked sweet potato (or 1 cup canned pumpkin)

1 cup wheat bran

2 eggs

¾ cup buttermilk

½ cup dark molasses

⅓ cup granulated or brown sugar

1¼ cups whole-wheat flour

2 teaspoons baking powder

½ teaspoon baking soda

1 teaspoon ground cinnamon

1 teaspoon ground ginger

1 cup dried cranberries

½ cup pumpkin seeds

fig bread

¾ cup orange juice

1 cup dried figs (any kind),
halved, with tips removed

½ cup sugar

2 tablespoons olive oil

1 tablespoon orange zest

2 eggs

1 cup flour

½ cup whole-wheat flour

1½ teaspoon baking soda

½ teaspoon salt

⅓ cup toasted crushed pecans,
plus ¼ cup for topping

With black tea, this is a sure sure sure thing (*i.e.*, figs + caffeine = go!).

MAKES ONE LOAF

Grease a 1-pound loaf pan. Microwave orange juice in glass container for 1 minute. Drop figs in hot orange juice to soak. Meanwhile, preheat oven to 350°F, and combine wet ingredients in one bowl and dry ingredients in another. Mix the orange juice and halved figs into wet ingredients, then fold into dry ingredients. Fill loaf pan. Sprinkle extra pecans on top. Bake for 45 minutes. Test with toothpick. Cool for at least 15 minutes before turning out of pan. Then cool another hour before serving, unless you don't mind it falling apart—in which case, eat it hot.

blackberry-banana boy-does-that-move-me muffins

If you need more than the name to encourage you to make these, I suggest brewing a cup of strong coffee, waking up, and trying to remember the last time you spent quality time in the loo.

MAKES A DOZEN

Preheat oven to 375°F. Grease a 12-cup muffin tin. Mix dry ingredients in one bowl. In another bowl, whisk together wet ingredients. Pour wet ingredients into dry ingredients, and stir until combined. Spoon batter into muffin cups. Bake for 20–25 minutes, or until a toothpick inserted in the center comes out clean. Wait 10 minutes, then turn muffins out of pan and cool on wire rack.

1½ cups whole-wheat flour

½ cup oat bran

½ cup ground pecans

½ cup brown sugar

2 teaspoons baking powder

1 teaspoon baking soda

½ teaspoon salt

2 cups ripe bananas, mashed

2 eggs

⅔ cup buttermilk

4 tablespoons butter, melted

½ cup blackberries (fresh or frozen)

buttermilk multi-grain waffles

¼ cup pumpkin seeds

6 tablespoons butter (plus 1 tablespoon)

1½ cups barley flour

¼ cup cornmeal

¼ cup oat flour

1 tablespoon packed brown sugar

1½ teaspoons baking powder

1 teaspoon ground cinnamon

¼ teaspoon baking soda

½ teaspoon salt

2 large eggs, lightly beaten

1¾ cups buttermilk

OPTIONAL TOPPINGS:

1 cup mixed fresh fruit

½ cup yogurt

½ cup warm maple syrup

½ cup Rhubarb Sauce (page 178)

Worth the extra effort. This batter will last a week in your refrigerator, and these waffles are so much more interesting than toast.

**MAKES 12–15 PANCAKES,
OR ABOUT 6 WAFFLES**

In a small skillet, heat pumpkin seeds over medium heat, tossing regularly until brown, for about 5 minutes. Pour seeds onto plate and set aside. Melt 6 tablespoons butter in a glass bowl in the microwave (about 1 minute, if frozen) or on stovetop, and set aside.

Mix dry ingredients and wet ingredients in separate medium-sized bowls. Fold wet into dry ingredients. Add melted butter. Preheat a griddle for pancakes and add the remaining butter, or coat a waffle iron with butter and turn it on. Make pancakes to desired size; if making waffles, spoon in enough batter to cover three-fourths of the iron. Pancakes will take about 7 minutes total. Waffles should be crisp and golden brown, 4 to 5 minutes.

BARLEY

Like other whole grains, barley is high in fiber. But its fiber is special: intestinal bacteria can break it down into butyric acid, which nourishes the cells of the large intestine. Barley also contains lots of selenium, which protects against colon cancer. It's worth noting that barley was the prune of the sixteenth century. Ptisan, a barley water drink, was "greatly disglueing and makes you joyful," according to Alexander Petronius, a Roman doctor of the 1580s.

corn cakes

¾ cup masa flour

3 whole eggs

½ cup cream

6 cups fresh or frozen corn kernels (about 8 ears, to be safe)

2 green onions, thinly sliced

1 teaspoon baking powder

1 teaspoon salt

Pepper, to taste

Olive oil

OPTIONAL TOPPINGS:

Smoked salmon, dill, and crème fraîche

Sour cream

Caviar

Maple syrup

My mother loves everything her cateress, Joan Prime, has ever brought to the house. Last year, she asked Joan to make something wheat free so the gluten-intolerant among her guests could enjoy more food. Joan complied and arrived with this doozy. Talk about a tactile wonderland in your mouth. What I love is that you can go upscale or downtown with these—add caviar and crème fraîche, or syrup. If you want more whole kernels visible, don't blend for very long during stage two. Also, you can make mini-corn cakes for hors d'oeuvres, or make them jumbo-sized for breakfast. The batter can be made up to two days ahead. It makes a lot, so invite lots of guests. This also makes a nice accompaniment to roast pork or grilled steak.

MAKES TWO DOZEN 4-INCH CAKES

Place masa flour, eggs, cream, and 3 cups corn kernels in the bowl of a food processor (or use a hand-held immersion blender) and process until smooth. Add remaining corn and process for a few seconds. There should still be some whole corn kernels. Transfer to a mixing bowl. Add green onions, baking powder, salt, and pepper. Heat a heavy skillet or griddle and coat with olive oil. When hot, use a

1-ounce measure to scoop up batter, and place onto the griddle. Separate cakes by about an inch to prevent their running into each other. Cook until nicely brown, then flip over and brown other side, about 4 minutes per side.

coconut cornbread

1 cup unsweetened coconut

1 cup course cornmeal

½ cup oat bran

½ cup whole-wheat pastry
flour

1 tablespoon baking powder

½ teaspoon salt

¼ cup brown sugar

1¼ cups coconut milk

2 eggs

4 ounces melted butter

I'm a cornbread fiend. I like it blue or yellow, dense or fluffy. The coconut here gives it a tropical air, and the bran gives it wings to fly.

SERVES 6

Preheat oven to 400°F. Toast coconut in 9-inch round skillet over low heat, tossing frequently to avoid burning. Set coconut aside, once browned. Let skillet cool, as you will use it later to bake the bread. Meanwhile, stir together dry ingredients in a large bowl. In a separate bowl, whisk together wet ingredients. Pour wet ingredients into dry ingredients. Add coconut, and mix well. Grease the cooled skillet with butter and pour in batter. Bake about 20 minutes, until top is set. Turn on broiler and broil for 1 minute to darken and crack top, watching carefully to avoid burning. Allow to cool in skillet for 10 minutes, and then turn out on a rack to cool.

OAT BRAN

If you were alive and reading newspapers in the 1980s, you probably remember the oat-bran craze. Oat bran was streaming out of the fountain of youth, saving us from heart attacks and other various and sundry death sentences. The craze blew over like a palm tree in Florida, but oat bran has not lost its magic powers. Particularly high in soluble fiber, it's somewhat gentler than wheat bran and absorbs water well, forming a creamy porridge when cooked. And, need we remind you, soluble fiber feeds the good bacteria in your gut.

APRICOTS

The apricot—meaning "early ripener" in Latin—is appropriately named. Ripe for only about eight weeks at the end of spring and start of summer, this little wonder-fruit has plenty to support a large fan base— fiber, beta-carotene, vitamin C, potassium, calcium, and phosphorus. First discovered growing wild in China, it made its way to America via the Spanish, who planted it at their missions. I'm sure it helped convert more than a few constipated heathens.

dried fig, apricot, and cherry compote over yogurt

My dad and I are dried-fruit fiends. He can eat all kinds and doesn't really need the help they provide. I hold that against him...The following is a reliable combination of fruits, but if you've got dried pears or dried peaches lying around, toss 'em in. The more, the merrier. Some people add sugar, but I don't think it's necessary. Don't skimp on the booze, however.

1½ cups dried Calimyrna figs, cut in half

1½ cups dried apricots, cut in half

1 cup dried sweet cherries

¾ cup sweet sherry

1 tablespoon orange zest

½ cup orange juice

Water, to cover

Cinnamon stick or ¼ teaspoon whole cloves (optional)

MAKES ABOUT 8 HALF-CUP SERVINGS

Put all of the ingredients in a medium saucepan and bring the mixture to a boil. Simmer uncovered for 30 minutes, or until the liquid sticks to the back of a spoon (like syrup). Cool in fridge for 2 hours. Serve over yogurt (or ice cream, if it's evening). For an added kick, sprinkle with pistachios or walnuts. Should keep for days (or even weeks) in your fridge.

dried apricots with goat cheese and pistachios

4 ounces *spreadable goat cheese*

12 *dried apricots*

½ cup *roasted, unsalted pistachios*

If you're anything like me, you like to shake up breakfast so it's not the same old whole-wheat toast with jam/peanut-butter/hummus/cream-cheese thingamajig you've been eating every day of your adult life. You also need something that doesn't take tons of prep time, and that, if accidentally photographed by an out-of-town guest, would make you appear the hilt of sophistication. This is it—the perfect melding of creamy and sweet. I prefer unsulfured apricots, but they're not nearly as pretty as the alternative; if you've got no problem with sulfur (it makes me wheeze), any dried apricots will do. Get spreadable goat cheese. I like Bucheron, but pick your favorite. Save yourself some hassle and buy shelled pistachios. This makes a lovely nibble for a brunch with friends, too. Just double or triple it. Figure 6 apricots per eater. I save my leftovers for the next day to dress up my drab toast concoction.

A LIGHT BREAKFAST FOR TWO

Smear a dab of goat cheese onto each apricot (the open side). Sprinkle with whole or chopped pistachios (press them into the cheese a bit, so they stick).

yogurt smoothies
two ways

Smoothies are the milkshake of the morning hours. But lots of smoothie fans miss out on the opportunity to make the drink a true mover and shaker. The added dash of wheat germ or flax is essential. And you'll barely notice the bonus fiber presence...at least on your tongue.

MANGO, BLACKBERRY, AND WHEAT GERM SMOOTHIE:

2 cups chopped mango

1 cup frozen or fresh blackberries

1 cup pineapple juice, frozen into ice cubes (about 4 cubes)

1 cup plain yogurt (or kefir)

½ cup wheat germ

2-3 ice cubes

Juice of 2 limes

MAKES ABOUT 2 PINTS OR ENOUGH FOR 4 SERVINGS

The prep method is the same for both. Pull out your blender. If it's an old blender and doesn't chop ice well, then crush your pineapple cubes and ice cubes in advance. (I like the freezer-bag, frying-pan method myself.) Blend all ingredients until smooth. Serve cold, with a sprig of mint if you have it. You can store any leftovers in your refrigerator, then re-freeze for half an hour before serving (you can re-blend, too, if you're so inclined).

PAPAYA, BANANA, AND FLAX MEAL SMOOTHIE:

2 cups peeled, seeded, chopped papaya

1 cup frozen banana

1 cup pineapple juice, frozen into ice cubes (about 4 cubes)

1 cup plain yogurt (or kefir)

½ cup flax meal

2-3 ice cubes

Juice of 2 limes

nut shake

At first taste—sweet, rich, and smooth—it seems like the sort of shake you could polish off in a few good slugs. But don't be fooled. You will want to sip slowly, and drinking more than a cup at one sitting is not advised. Powerful stuff.

¾ cup roasted almonds or cashews

5 dried dates

½ teaspoon vanilla extract

1 cup apple juice

3 frozen bananas

½–1 cup whole milk yogurt

MAKES ABOUT 5 HALF-PINT GLASSES

Soak the nuts in water for 1 hour. At the same time, soak the dates in water for 1 hour. Drain and dump the nut water, but reserve the nuts. Drain and keep the date water. Combine the nuts, dates, date water, vanilla, and apple juice; process until smooth. Cut in frozen bananas and yogurt. Add water or yogurt and reblend as needed to make smooth.

FIBER ON ICE

Despite their fibrous natures, fruit smoothies and nut shakes would not have received endorsements from Mr. and Mrs. Kellogg back in the 1890s, when they dominated the constipation scene:

"If cold foods or drinks are taken with the meal, such as ice cream, ice water, iced milk, or tea, the stomach is chilled, and a long delay in the digestive process is occasioned."

Ella Eaton Kellogg (a founding member of the Kellogg's Corn Flakes family), *Science in the Kitchen. A Scientific Treatise on Food Substances and their Dietetic Properties, Together with a Practical Explanation of the Principles of Healthful Cookery, and a Large Number of Original, Palatable, and Wholesome Recipes,* 1893

hot millet with dried fruit

1 ½ cups water

2 cups milk

1 pinch of salt

1 cup hulled millet

1 tablespoon butter

¼ cup mixed chopped nuts

1 tablespoon honey

¼ cup dried fruit (unsulfured)

½ cup yogurt or kefir

In remote parts of Cameroon, West Africa, there is very little incidence of colon cancer or any of its related illnesses (colitis, ulcers, reflux, etc.). According to Dr. Daphne Miller, author of *The Jungle Effect: A Doctor Discovers the Healthiest Diets from Around the World—Why They Work and How to Bring Them Home*. Miller is all about using diet to heal her San Franciscoan patients, so when she found out about the healthy guts in Cameroon, she trekked to sub-Saharan Africa to inspect their pantries and see what was keeping local guts so happy. What did she find? The Five Fs—fiber, folate, fermented food, foraged food, and less flesh. This recipe has almost all the Fs going for it. Here's my adaptation of Miller's approach to West African breakfast grub.

SERVES 4

In a medium saucepan, combine the water, milk, and salt. Using medium heat, bring to almost a boil (the surface will begin to steam, but you shouldn't see bubbles). Meanwhile, place millet in a small sauté pan and toast on medium heat, stirring occasionally, until fragrant, about 5 minutes (the grains will pop; fear not). When millet is still hot, add it to the water, milk, and salt. Reduce to a simmer

and cook, covered, 20 to 30 minutes, stirring occasionally to avoid scorching. The millet should be
soft and creamy in appearance. Add butter and stir
until melted. Serve hot in cereal bowls with copious
amounts of toppings: nuts, honey, dried fruit, and
yogurt or kefir.

MILLET

Traditionally prepared in a fermented porridge called
ogi, millet is also a delicious addition to baked goods,
adding a light, crunchy texture and a warm, nutty flavor. It has many of the benefits of whole grains, from
high fiber to magnificent mineral content. The medieval
Tacuinum of Paris tells us that millet is "good for those
who wish to refresh the stomach and dry out superflu-
ous humors."

fried eggs with salsa and corn tortillas

1 (15-ounce) can black beans
or your favorite canned beans

8 fresh Corn Tortillas (page 124)

8 eggs

¼ cup low-fat milk

2 ounces butter

1 cup shredded sharp cheddar

½ cup fresh Corn Salsa (page
54 or store bought)

OPTIONAL TOPPINGS:

1 avocado, sliced

½ cup sour cream

I, for one, swear by eggs, but I can't find any con-
temporary literature to support my theory that they
move through us like rakes through leaves. In fact,
all I could find was 200-year-old literature that warns
diners to avoid eggs when constipated. But who really knows. To hedge the bet, have them with spicy
salsa, beans, and fresh corn tortillas.

SERVES 4

Do I really need to tell you how to prepare this? OK,
for the true beginner, first, preheat your oven to 450°F.
Next, get your beans going in a small saucepan; turn
heat to medium and cover. When the oven is ready,
place your tortillas on a baking sheet and slide into
oven. I like my tortillas crispy, so this is my method.
They will take about 7 minutes. Next, crack eggs into
a bowl. Whisk for 40 seconds. Add milk. Whisk again.
Place large skillet on stove. Heat butter in skillet, on
high heat. (Stir your beans if you haven't recently.)
When butter is bubbly and coats skillet, pour in eggs.
As eggs cook, push cooked bits into the center of the
pan and let runny, uncooked egg flow to the edges.
Add cheese to eggs (or, if you prefer, add it to the
beans), turn down heat to warm, cover skillet, and
wait another 1 to 2 minutes for cheese to melt. Pull

tortillas from oven. To serve, layer ingredients in this order: tortilla, beans, and eggs, with salsa on top. If you're feeling decadent, slice up some avocado and serve with a dollop of sour cream.

EGGS

Eggs are one of those foods about which you will hear all kinds of contradictory information, and these contradictions go way back. From William Tibbles's *Dietetics; Or, Food in Health and Disease,* written in 1914: "Boiled eggs or hard-boiled eggs are considered constipating, but buttered eggs or scrambled eggs are laxative by reason of the fat used in cooking. Boiled eggs are not constipating to everybody. There are some people who are purged by the yolk of one egg." This yo-yo analysis hasn't improved much in 100 years. Needless to say, this is one of those foods that makes the "key" list because of an abundance of anecdotal cheerleading.

homemade granola

6 cups rolled oats

1 cup slivered almonds
(walnuts, cashews, or pecans
work too)

1 cup dried shredded coconut
(unsweetened)

¾ cup honey

½ cup sesame seeds

½ cup pumpkin seeds

1 teaspoon cinnamon

¼ teaspoon salt

1 cup dried cranberries (or any
other chopped, dried fruit)

With good granola costing upwards of $8 a bag, I don't see why more people don't make their own. It's easy and keeps practically forever in the fridge, where it can be a perpetual source of excitement in the morning.

ABOUT 16 SERVINGS

Preheat oven to 350°F. Combine all ingredients, except fruit, in a large bowl. Spread mixture over large cookie sheet (with sides). Bake for 20 minutes. Pull out of oven and carefully toss—with wooden spoons—moving darker bits into the middle and less dark bits out toward the corners. Return to oven for another 15 to 20 minutes, until mixture is nicely browned. Keep a close eye on it to avoid burning. Your home should smell like a bakery when the granola is ready. Remove from oven, toss in the dried fruit, and let cool. Refrigerate in sealable container when totally cool. Should keep for months. Serve with plain yogurt to make it a 10 on the Go-Meter.

grilled yogurt cheese and honey on whole-wheat bâtard

SERVES UP TO 6 (2 SLICES PER PERSON), DEPENDING ON SIZE OF BREAD

This is a no-brainer. I won't even bother with the formalities of an ingredient list. Buy your favorite whole-wheat loaf. I like the oval bâtard, but get whatever yummy, fresh-baked, whole-grain bread you can get your hands on (good excuse to go for a walk first thing in the morning and get the guts moving anyway). Cut into thick slices and toast to desired darkness. Immediately layer on yogurt cheese (buy about 8 ounces). Let the heat from the warm toast soften the cheese slightly. Serve. A drizzle of honey on top makes a nice treat for those with a sweet tooth.

lox and cultured cream cheese on seeded rye

8 slices seeded rye or
pumpernickel bread

½ cup cultured cream cheese

1 teaspoon dry dill

8 ounces lox (I like dry-
smoked, flaky lox)

1 large tomato, sliced

½ red onion, sliced thin

2 small pickling cucumbers

¼ cup capers

1 avocado, sliced

This is too easy, but I have to include it since it's a breakfast staple. Too many miss the opportunity to make it a mover because they insist on bagels (Satan spawn for the gut) and plain old cream cheese, when they could substitute seeded rye or pumpernickel and cultured cream cheese, and win, win, win.

SERVES 4 BIG EATERS
OR 8 LITTLE ONES

In case you're not familiar with this Jewish breakfast staple, here's how to organize the ingredients. First, toast your bread; the easiest way is to pop all those slices in a 425°F oven on a baking sheet for 5 minutes or so, until slightly crisp. Meanwhile, put your other ingredients on platters or in nice ramekins and arrange on a table or buffet. When the toast is ready, stack on a plate and add to the offerings. The optimal order of ingredients is toast slathered with cream cheese, and topped with dill, lox, tomato, onion, cucumber, capers, and—if you're from California, or wish you were—avocado. Some people like this open-faced, but for less mess, finish the sandwich with another slice of bread.

RYE FOR ROYALTY

In 1608 Nicholas Abraham, French nobleman and future counselor to King Louis XIII, wrote of the promising nature of roughage. Some roughage is good and some bad, he said, depending on the person. He was particularly fond of roughage in the form of rye, and prescribed rye bread to lords at court to give the stomach "looseness." He also noted that rye eaten by the women of Lyons made their bodies robust and succulent, roughly translated…

snacks, dips, and spreads

Santorio Santorio, an Italian food scientist of the 1600s, was one of the first to conduct experiments on himself to determine the nutritional values of different foods. His method was to weigh himself before and after eating, and then to weigh his "business." When the numbers didn't quite work out (e.g., an ounce of cheese going in did not equal an ounce of cheese coming out), he came up with the theory of "insensible perspiration."

spanikopita with chard

1 tablespoon olive oil

1 medium yellow onion, diced

1½ pounds clean, dry Swiss chard, stems removed

½ teaspoon salt for chard, plus ½ teaspoon salt for cheese mix

⅓ cup crumbled feta cheese

⅓ cup cottage cheese

2 eggs, lightly beaten

2 tablespoons chopped fresh dill or 1 tablespoon dill weed

2 tablespoons chopped fresh mint

1 teaspoon black pepper

1 roll frozen phyllo dough, thawed

4 tablespoons unsalted butter, melted

A twist on the more traditional version (which uses spinach), this three-sided dumpling will impress friends, astound family, and then race its way to your "finish" line.

SERVES 4

Place the olive oil in a large sauté pan over medium-high heat. Add onion and sauté about 5 minutes, until slightly limp. Chop chard into ribbons and add to onion with salt. It may not all fit at once; as the chard closest to the flame wilts, more room will become available. Toss frequently. When fully cooked, the greens will appear bright green. Cooking may take 5 to 8 minutes. Transfer the chard to a colander and drain. Set aside.

In the same sauté pan, use a wooden spoon to blend feta, cottage cheese, eggs, dill weed, and mint. Season with ½ teaspoon salt and ½ teaspoon black pepper.

When chard is cool enough to handle, wrap in a dish towel or several layers of paper towels, and squeeze out moisture. Add to cheese mix, using your hands to incorporate.

Heat oven to 375°F. Unroll phyllo and place 1 sheet on a clean work surface (cover the remaining stack of phyllo with plastic wrap or a damp towel to keep it from drying out). Brush phyllo sheet with melted butter and top with a second sheet. Brush the second sheet with butter and top with a third sheet. Cut the phyllo in half lengthwise to get two strips, each about 3 by 13 inches.

Put about 3 tablespoons of cheese–chard filling on the base of one of the strips. Fold up the phyllo as you would a flag, creating a triangular package. Place triangle on a parchment-lined baking sheet and brush with butter. Repeat with the remaining phyllo.

Ingredients should make 6 to 7 triangles. There may be leftover phyllo, but there shouldn't be leftover filling. Bake the triangles until golden brown, about 20 to 25 minutes.

RAISINS

"Strengthen me with raisins and refresh me with apples because I am weak from love." That's from Song of Solomon 2:5. Is there anything more to add? Even God endorses raisins. If you care to be clever, call them what they are: dried grapes. After prunes, they're the other go-to fruit for the health media machine.

marinated dried fruit (or if it's passover and you're jewish: haroset)

Some people save haroset for Passover, but that limits it to eight days a year and the Jews. Why should one group get to hog what might be God's greatest gift to the gut? Eat with matzo if you must (see the Corkage chapter—pg 227—for more on matzo) or spoon over seed-covered crackers with a chunk of sharp cheese. This is the Sephardic style of haroset, meaning it has Middle Eastern origins as opposed to European— more flavor, deeper colors, and more effective.

½ cup pitted, chopped Medjool
   dates
¼ cup chopped golden raisins
½ cup sweet red wine
½ cup chopped dried apricots
¼ cup chopped dried figs
½ cup chopped apple
⅓ cup orange juice
½ cup chopped walnuts

SERVES 6 AS A LIGHT APPETIZER

Cover dates and raisins with wine and let sit for at least 8 hours in sealed glass container. When ready, add apricots, figs, apple, and juice. Right before serving, add walnuts. Mix with spoon.

bacon-wrapped dates

20 *dates, pitted, preferably*
  Medjool
10 *slices bacon*
20 *toothpicks*

I think of this appetizer and conjure an unattractive picture. Do yourself a favor—don't conjure, just cook and eat. There's no way to make this pretty. That said, this is palate wonderland. Splurge on good bacon. Serve at a family function like Memorial Day or the Fourth of July, when you've only got your family to impress. They'll thank you the next day, if not before.

SERVES 6

Cut each bacon slice in half (so it's half as long). Preheat oven to 450°F. Wrap each date with one of the halved bacon slices. Use a toothpick to hold bacon in place. Place wrapped dates on baking sheet with plenty of separation between each. Cook for 10 minutes, then flip and bake until second side is crispy. Serve. Note: Before baking, some truly decadent folks like to stuff their figs with goat cheese or gorgonzola for added flavor (if you go this route, keep an eye on the cheese as it cooks; you don't want it getting too soft and runny). It's worth trying if you can afford the extra calories.

tamari nuts

Who said you can't get fiber, watch football, and still look cool?

2 cups raw unsalted nuts (cashews and almonds are best)

3 tablespoons tamari soy sauce

SERVES 6 AS A SNACK

Preheat oven to 350°F. Roast nuts on baking sheet for 5 minutes. Remove from oven, and pour tamari over the nuts, mixing with a wooden spoon so the sauce coats all the nuts. Return to oven and bake for another 5 minutes. Turn off the oven. Stir nuts and return to oven as oven cools down. This last step is key. The nuts are done when they are dry and crunchy in your mouth (as opposed to soft and chewy). When the nuts are totally cool, store in the fridge in sealed container.

pickles

Though cucumbers are not present on the key-foods list, fermented foods are, and when a cucumber soaks in water and salt long enough, it becomes a delicious fermented food called a pickle. According to the doctors I've talked to, when the bacteria from that pickle hits your gut, it kickstarts your colon like a dead car battery shocked with live wires. You could just as easily soak and ferment cauliflower, carrots, cabbage, green beans, asparagus, or pretty much any vegetable or fruit in your fridge. Cucumbers are just the most common (in the States, we eat approximately 20 billion pickles a year). I could spend this page teaching you to make your own pickles, but the reality is that a couple of serious connoisseurs in Canada and New York have perfected the art, and their products make the effort of prepping pickles at home sorta silly. Go to the pickle section of your grocery store and look for a label with three key ingredients—cucumber, water, salt—a few spices, and not much else.

If you see vinegar on the label, turn back. Vinegar pickles are not a fermented food and therefore not a food *The Un-Constipated Gourmet* would ever recommend. Vinegar pickles, the redheaded

stepchildren of pickles, don't grow bacteria because vinegar kills bacteria. That's why we use it
to clean ovens and wash windows.

FERMENTED FACTS

Sauerkraut, kimchi, and pickles will not cure every
ailment, but they will contribute to your overall well-
being. Live-culture (unpasteurized) fermented foods
improve digestion, absorption of nutrients (especially
minerals), and immune function. Fermenting vegetables
preserves them with their nutrients intact, "predigests"
those nutrients into more accessible forms, and gen-
erates *additional* nutrients, both vitamins and obscure
micronutrients only just beginning to be identified and
understood. What you get from local ferments is local
culture, quite literally—the unique community of mi-
crobial subspecies that inhabit a particular place. The local *Lactobacillus*, and the motley company it's found with,

replenish your gut microflora, which probably need regular replenishment, given the prevalence of broad-spectrum antibacterial chemicals. The particular lactobacilli that inhabit your environment are uniquely adapted to that particular place. There is no simpler way to invite these bacterial allies into our lives and share them with the people around us than by becoming food producers and fermenting some vegetables ourselves at home. A head of cabbage forgotten on an obscure shelf of your pantry will not spontaneously transform itself into sauerkraut. Vegetables left exposed to air start to grow molds, and if left long enough, those molds can reduce a head of cabbage to a puddle of slime, bearing no resemblance whatsoever to crunchy, delicious, and aromatic sauerkraut. The simple key to successful vegetable fermentation is to make sure your vegetables are submerged in liquid. That's it, the big secret.

Sandor Katz, The Revolution Will Not Be Microwaved, 2006

edamame with chili oil

Why does football have to pair with potato chips and hot dogs? Why can't it go with edamame and hot oil or fresh roasted tamari nuts? Go the latter culinary route, and you'll find yourself too busy—in the bathroom—to watch the half-time show.

1 (16-ounce) package shelled edamame

4 cups ice water

2 tablespoons sesame oil

4–5 tablespoons lime juice

½–1 teaspoon chili flakes

½–1 tablespoon salt

SERVES 4 AS A SNACK

Cook edamame (package directions will tell you how); it should still be bright green when you plunge it into ice water to cool them. Once cool, drain them and toss into bowl with sesame oil, lime juice, chili flakes, and salt (start with the lesser amounts of salt and chili and add more to suit your taste).

baby artichokes with parmesan

2 pounds baby artichokes

3 cups ice water

3 tablespoons lemon juice or white vinegar

½ cup olive oil

2 shallots, chopped

2 green onions (scallions), chopped, including the green ends

3 cloves garlic, minced

1 teaspoon chopped fresh thyme

1 teaspoon salt or more, to taste

Pepper, to taste

½ cup grated Parmesan cheese

While I want to give you recipes with artichokes, I don't want you to go through the frustration of boiling a big one for 40 minutes, only to discover that only 1/20th of it is actually edible; nor do I want you buying jars of artichokes, because they're gross. The only way to cook artichokes that makes sense to me is to sauté baby artichokes. Ninety percent of a baby artichoke is edible, because there's no fuzzy choke; and the outer leaves are much more tender. You can eat this dish warm or hot. You'll taste how fibrous this vegetable is, so I won't even go into my spiel about reasons to eat it.

SERVES 6 AS AN APPETIZER
OR 4 AS A SIDE DISH

Fill a bowl with 3 cups ice water; add 2 tablespoons lemon juice (or vinegar). Set aside. Groom each artichoke by cutting half an inch off the base, removing the top layer of leaves (potentially more, if the leaves remaining on the surface look thick and stiff), and cutting off the remaining sharp tips. Halve each artichoke and drop into the lemon (or vinegar) water. This helps the artichoke retain its color. After 5 minutes, drain artichokes. In a large sauté pan, heat 1 cup of water until it boils; add artichokes. Cover and simmer 4 minutes. Drain. In same pan (now empty), add oil. Once hot, add the artichokes, shallots, green onion, garlic, and thyme. Cook for five minutes, stirring occasionally. Add the remaining lemon juice (or vinegar), salt, and pepper. Arrange artichokes on a platter and sprinkle with Parmesan cheese.

ARTICHOKES

Your liver and gall bladder usually help with the digestion of fats. If your gall bladder isn't making enough bile, eating fats will constipate you. Artichokes stimulate the production of bile, relieving constipation of the sluggish-liver, miserly-gall-bladder variety. They also contain loads of fiber.

whole-wheat walnut bruschetta

1¼ cups cherry tomatoes, cut
into halves

¼ cup olive oil

4 garlic cloves (two cut in half,
two finely diced)

½ cup chopped basil

½ loaf whole-wheat bread
(I like mine with walnuts),
cut into ¾-inch-thick slices

Salt and pepper, to taste

Parmesan cheese (optional)

God bless the artisanal bakers who've figured out how to insert whole grains into their breads while maintaining the addictive textures and flavors. The bread does all the heavy lifting in this recipe, so be sure to invest in a good loaf. And don't skimp on cheap tomatoes here either. You will need sweet, fresh ones to counteract the garlic.

SERVES 4 AS AN APPETIZER

In medium glass bowl, marinate the tomatoes in olive oil, finely diced garlic, and basil for 10 minutes. Meanwhile, toast or grill bread slices until crispy; about 5 minutes (I like to do this in the oven on a cookie sheet; you may need to turn the bread once to get it toasty all over). Remove from heat and rub each slice with the halves of garlic (gently—don't break the bread). Spread a layer of marinated tomatoes over each slice. Season with salt and pepper. Serve on a platter. Optional: Dress with shaved Parmesan cheese.

LET US NOT REPEAT HISTORY...FOREVER

In the 1872 *American Woman's Home*, Harriet Beecher Stowe recounts a charming anecdote. A wheat shortage in Britain forced the army to serve its soldiers whole-grain bread. Suddenly, everyone marched briskly in step, chins high and eyes bright. The medics were shocked at such unprecedented health and vigor in the ranks. She wrote, "...The woody fiber is not digested, but serves by its bulk and stimulating action to facilitate digestion." After two years, everyone forgot why they felt so good and went back to white bread.

MANGOS

According to Ayurvedic medicine (a type of medicine practiced in India and followed by many yogis), ripe mangos help with the elimination of waste. They are rich in insoluble fiber and contain an enzyme with stomach-soothing properties similar to those found in papayas. An average-sized mango can contain up to 40 percent of your daily fiber requirement, and in many parts of the world, mangos are eaten whole, like peaches (i.e., hand to mouth, with juice running down the chin).

mango chutney

I think a lot of Americans don't know what to make of chutney, a staple of Indian food. Is it a jam? Is it a side dish? Is it dessert? Yes. All of the above. And a digestive, too.

2 teaspoons oil

2 large garlic cloves, minced

1 teaspoon grated ginger

2 cinnamon sticks

4 whole cloves

2 teaspoons chili powder (without salt)

2 peeled, pitted mangos, chopped

1 cup unseasoned rice vinegar

⅓ cup sugar

MAKES ABOUT 1½ CUPS

Heat the oil in a saucepan, and add garlic and ginger. Sauté until fragrant, about a minute, and then add cinnamon sticks, cloves, chili powder, mango, vinegar, and sugar. Stir. Bring to a boil, and simmer for about 30 minutes, stirring occasionally. Finished product should be lumpy, with a syrupy consistency (which you can test on the back of a spoon). Remove cloves and cinnamon before serving. Serve with cream cheese or goat cheese on flax-seed crackers, for best results.

tzatziki

2 cups Greek yogurt

2 small pickling cucumbers, chopped fine (if you want a less watery tzatziki, you can lightly salt the cukes now, and drain them over a colander for 15 minutes before adding to the other ingredients)

2 cloves garlic, minced

1 tablespoon olive oil

3 teaspoons white wine vinegar or white balsamic vinegar

2 teaspoons fresh dill

¼ teaspoon salt

Pepper, to taste

Some tzatziki recipes require you to seed and peel your cucumbers. That's because most of us are stuck using the waxy tasteless cucumbers in most grocery stores. However, if you have access to tasty organic pickling cucumbers, you should enjoy every bit of them, seeds and skin included. Find them at your nearby farmers' market, Whole Foods, or other specialty grocery stores.

SERVES 6

Combine all ingredients. Let sit in fridge for at least 1 hour, so flavors meld. Serve with lamb, steak, or Falafel (page 148).

CULTURED DAIRY

The yogurt craze may seem to be a modern phenomenon (Activia, etc.) but evidence of its zeitgeist comes as early as 1909, when a short book called *Soured Milk and Pure Cultures of Lactic Acid Bacilli in the Treatment of Disease* was published, proclaiming sour milk's antibiotic properties. Yogurt, sour milk, pills, etc., flooded the market.

James Whorton, Inner Hygiene

pesto three ways

2 cups basil leaves, packed

½ cup pine nuts or walnuts

5 large garlic cloves

½ cup grated Parmesan cheese

¼ cup olive oil

Salt and black pepper, to taste

ARUGULA PESTO:

2 cups packed arugula leaves

½ cup toasted walnuts

5 garlic cloves

½ cup fresh Parmesan cheese

¼ cup extra-virgin olive oil

Salt and black pepper, to taste

CILANTRO PESTO:

3 cups cilantro

1½ cups parsley

½ cup pine nuts or walnuts,
  toasted

2 scallions

8 garlic cloves

3 teaspoons fresh lemon or lime
  juice

½ cup olive oil

Salt and cayenne pepper, to taste

The Greeks believe that olive oil is the cure for most things, including the slow gut. Pesto is a terrific vehicle for olive oil. Here are three ways to make it. The basil version works best on pasta; the arugula is dynamite smeared on baguette slices; and the cilantro is a terrific sauce tossed over warm roasted potatoes or vegetables.

MAKES ABOUT A CUP

Place all ingredients, except for salt and pepper, in blender. Blend. If pesto looks dry, add an extra 2 tablespoons oil. Blend again until pesto appears pasty. Season with salt and pepper. Store in tightly sealed container. Use within a week, or freeze.

baba ganoush

Michael Lukas, writer and former assistant to Jewish-cookbook author Joan Nathan, was traveling in Turkey on a Fulbright scholarship when nature called. And called. And called. But no one answered. "Turkey is not the best place for the gastrointestinally challenged," according to Lukas. "With a meat- and bread-heavy cuisine, and an emphasis on hot peppers, it can trouble even the strongest stomachs." One day, after a week of stasis, he attended a potluck. He brought a traditional Turkish appetizer, baba ganoush, or *patlican salatisa*, as the Turks call it. "In the back of my mind I thought the mixture of roasted eggplant and yogurt might help unclog my plumbing." A few days before, he'd tried drinking olive oil at the suggestion of his Turkish roommate. It didn't work. The baba ganoush did...

1 large eggplant

Juice of 2 lemons

¼ cup tahini

3 cloves garlic, crushed

2 tablespoons chopped parsley

2 tablespoons olive oil

1 teaspoon salt

1 tablespoon chopped cilantro

SERVES 6 AS AN APPETIZER

Roast the eggplant under the broiler or on the grill, turning a few times until the skin is black and blistered. When cool enough, peel off skin, and squeeze out juice. Blend eggplant flesh in processor with the lemon juice, tahini, garlic, 1 tablespoon of parsley, and olive oil. Purée until smooth. Add salt and blend again.

Sprinkle remaining parsley and cilantro over top. Serve in a ramekin with carrot sticks or cucumber slices. Excellent on Falafel (page 148).

white bean dip
with cilantro

I think of this as the Latino version of hummus.

SERVES 8 AS AN APPETIZER

Process all ingredients in blender except for 2 tablespoons of cilantro, which are saved for garnish. For added "go," serve with thick tortilla chips or homemade whole-wheat croutons (essentially thinly sliced, heavily toasted bread, with olive oil and garlic rubbed in).

3 (15-ounce) cans cannellini beans, rinsed and drained

¾ cup olive oil (maybe more)

½ cup minced fresh cilantro

3 tablespoons fresh lemon juice

3 garlic cloves

3 teaspoons ground cumin

2 teaspoons chili powder

Salt and pepper, to taste

CHICKPEAS

Culpeper writes in his magnificent *Herbal* that chickpeas are "less windy than beans" but nonetheless "move the belly downwards." We should know—humans have been cultivating them for some ten thousand years. They're absolutely chock-full of nutrition, with large quantities of calcium and manganese, and, of course, fiber—both soluble and insoluble. Chickpeas also travel under the alias garbanzo beans.

hummus

Everybody knows that hummus is the big sister of baba ganoush, so it would feel slightly odd to include one and not the other here—especially since their efficacy is doubled when you dive into both at once. The trick is NOT eating them with pita, which is a member of the Ten Plagues of the Gut. Instead, try carrots, cucumbers, or Falafel (page 148).

SERVES 6

Soak chickpeas overnight. Drain and cover with fresh water. Bring to a simmer and cook until tender, about one hour. Drain, reserving liquid, and let cool. Measure 2 cups of cooked chickpeas and place in the blender or food processor with the tahini, lemon juice, garlic, and ½ cup of the reserved cooking liquid. (If you have more than 2 cups of chickpeas after soaking, consider using them for Safsoof, page 81; don't wait more than 2 days to use them, as they'll start to ferment in your refrigerator.) Purée until smooth. Drizzle in the olive oil and purée until shiny and smooth. Add paprika and salt, to taste. Serve sprinkled with paprika and drizzled with olive oil.

   *A note from the creator, Rosanna, "This hummus is on the subtle side of garlic and the nutty side of sesame."

1 cup dry chickpeas

¼ cup plus 1 tablespoon tahini

¼ cup lemon juice (about 1 large lemon's worth)

1 clove garlic

¼ cup extra-virgin olive oil

¼ teaspoon paprika (smoked is delicious), or to taste

1 teaspoon salt, or to taste

hot corn-papaya salsa with thick tortilla chips

1½ pounds sweet tomatoes, diced

1 cup barely cooked corn kernels, cut from cob

1 cup papaya, chopped (leave out if you're using this with fish tacos)

¾ cup finely chopped onion

¼ cup chopped fresh cilantro leaves

2 tablespoons fresh lime juice

2 tablespoons seeded, minced jalapeno or serrano chiles

1 teaspoon minced garlic

½ teaspoon salt

Though you won't find hot peppers on our key foods list, it's well documented (at least by me) that hot food moves food. But if you want to give the credit to the papaya and corn, fine.

SERVES 4

Gently toss all ingredients in a glass bowl. Let sit for at least 1 hour before serving. Serve with thick (store-bought) tortilla chips, guacamole, and beer. Also perfect with Black Bean Soup (page 60), Bean Cakes (page 150), and Fish Tacos (page 164).

PAPAYAS

Among devotees, it's common knowledge that papayas aid digestion, but it amazes me how few people actually eat them in my urban world. A digestive aid inherent to the fruit—papain—breaks down protein and cleanses the digestive track, meaning faster metabolism and less fat lingering around. Yes, that means dieters with a sweet tooth should be gobbling this fruit instead of diet soda. Papaya also delivers a nutritional kick—vitamin C, folate, potassium, fiber, vitamin A, vitamin E, and lycopene. Some folks find the golden flesh of ripe papaya a little slimy; if that's the case with you, throw it into a smoothie or salsa to reduce the texture conflict. Note: Its center cavity is packed with black seeds, which, I'm told, are edible and probably relieve some mysterious medical condition that modern medicine has yet to sort out.

soups

"Foods should be given which leave a bulky residue, as the passing of this through the intestines stimulates peristaltic action. Oils should be used. MAY TAKE soups—broths, oyster soup, sorrel soup."

Edwin Charles French, Food for the Sick and How to Prepare It:
with a Chapter on Food for the Baby (Morton, Louisville) 1900

BAD BREATH, GOOD GUTS?

"Onions, garlic, leeks, chives and shallot,* all of which are similar, possess medicinal virtues of a marked character, stimulating the circulatory system and the consequent increase of the saliva and the gastric juice promoting digestion...A soup made from onions is regarded by the French as an excellent restorative in debility of the digestive organs."

Hugo Ziemann, Steward of the White House, and Mrs. F.L. Gillette, *The White House Cook Book, A Comprehensive Cyclopedia of Information for the Home Containing Cooking, Toilet and Household Recipes, Menus, Dinner-Giving, Table Etiquette, Care of the Sick, Health Suggestions, Facts Worth Knowing, etc.* (The Saalfield Publishing Co, NY) 1905.

* Though onions, garlic, leeks, chives, and shallots do not appear on the key foods list, I find it interesting that presidents have relied on them in the past.

tuscan bean soup

For best flavor, make a day before you want to eat it, and invest in real (not poseur domestic) Parmigiano, or you're cheating yourself of the true effect.

SERVES 4 AS A MAIN AND
6 AS A STARTER

Place 2 tablespoons olive oil in a large soup pot over high heat. When oil is hot, add the garlic, onions, carrots, celery, leeks, and chili pepper. Sauté for 2 minutes. Add salt and pepper. Add hock. Sauté for 1 minute. Add the presoaked beans, rosemary, thyme, and bay leaf. Cook for 1 minute. Add stock and bring to a boil. Reduce to a simmer. Cook for about 2 hours. Beans should be tender. Remove hock, thyme sprigs, and bay leaves. Use an immersion blender to purée the soup, about 30 seconds. It should not be completely blended. Pick the meat from the ham hock and chop roughly; return meat to soup. Add dashes of salt and pepper, to taste.

In a sauté pan, heat the remaining olive oil. Add 2 crushed garlic cloves and chopped thyme and simmer for 1 minute. This infuses the oil with flavor. Turn off heat; discard garlic cloves. Stir infused olive oil into the soup. Garnish individual bowls with chopped parsley and Parmigiano cheese.

2 tablespoons plus ¼ cup olive oil

1½ tablespoons chopped garlic

1 cup minced onions

1 carrot, chopped

1 celery stalk, chopped

½ cup finely chopped leeks, white part only

½ hot chili pepper, stem removed, minced

1 teaspoon salt

1 teaspoon pepper

1 (3-4 ounce) ham hock

½ pound white beans, soaked at least 12 hours, drained

1 tablespoon minced rosemary

2 sprigs thyme

1 bay leaf

5 cups chicken stock

2 large garlic cloves, crushed

1 teaspoon chopped thyme

½ cup grated Parmigiano cheese

½ cup chopped fresh parsley

black bean soup with fresh herbs

2 tablespoons olive oil

1 large onion, peeled and chopped

1 large carrot, peeled and chopped

4 large garlic cloves, minced

2 teaspoons ground cumin

1–2 teaspoons chopped jalapeño with seeds

2 (15-ounce) cans black beans, undrained

1 cup diced tomatoes

1½ cups low-salt chicken broth

Salt and pepper, to taste

OPTIONAL TOPPINGS:

1 cup chopped fresh cilantro

1 cup chopped green onions

1 cup crumbled goat cheese or queso fresco

Corn Salsa (page 54)

Avocado, sliced

Sour cream

The kids have a festive song about beans that you're probably aware of; perhaps you even sang it yourself in grade school to earn a few laughs. The properties of these fibrous legumes are that legendary. This recipe happens to deliver a double wallop. Spices—particularly the ones packing heat—will also benefit the Unconstipated Gourmet. I like to serve this with a hearty Coconut Cornbread (page 12) and honey butter.

SERVES 4 AS AN ENTREE
OR 6 AS A STARTER

Place oil in a large soup pot over medium-high heat. Add the onion, carrot, and garlic, and sauté until vegetables begin to soften, about 6 minutes. Mix in cumin and 1 teaspoon jalapeño. Add the beans, tomatoes with juice, and broth, and bring soup to a boil. Reduce heat to medium, cover, and cook until carrots are tender, about 15 minutes. It's up to you if you want to blend this soup or enjoy its original texture. If you want to blend it, an immersion (stick) blender works best. After blending, simmer another 15 minutes. Season to taste with salt, pepper, and remaining 1 teaspoon jalapeño (if you like it hot). Ladle soup into bowls. Pass cilantro, green onions, and cheese. For extra color, pass around salsa, sliced avocado, and sour cream.

pea soup with ham hock

An American staple for a reason...

**SERVES 4 AS A MAIN OR
6 AS A STARTER**

Heat oil in a soup pot. Add onions, carrots, and celery, stirring frequently, until vegetables begin to brown. Reduce heat to medium-low and add butter and garlic. Cook another minute. Then add potatoes, ham hock, peas, water, stock, and bay leaves. Bring to a boil, and then simmer for about 2 hours, until peas become mushy. Skim frothy fat off the top, if you're so inclined. Season with salt, pepper, and thyme (you probably won't need a lot of salt). Carefully remove ham bone and set on cutting board; using large fork and knife, cut off and shred meat. Discard bone and remove bay leaves. Return meat to soup. Stir. Cook another 5 minutes, then ladle soup into bowls. Note: Leftovers may need a bit of extra water or stock, as the soup thickens in the refrigerator.

2 tablespoons extra-virgin olive oil

2 medium onions, chopped medium

2 medium carrots, chopped medium

2 medium stalks celery, chopped medium

1 tablespoon unsalted butter

2 teaspoons minced garlic

3 red potatoes, diced

1 ham bone (hock or other) with plenty of good meat on it

2½ cups split peas, rinsed

4 cups water

4 cups chicken stock

4 bay leaves

1 teaspoon dried thyme

Salt and pepper, to taste

dal

1 cup split pigeon pea lentils
(yellow)

3 tomatoes (medium-sized)

1 teaspoon turmeric powder

1 teaspoon salt

½ teaspoon paprika or ground
red pepper

2 tablespoons corn or canola oil

1 teaspoon fenugreek seeds

1 teaspoon mustard seeds (dark
red or bleached)

1 tablespoon sugar (optional)

Additional salt and pepper, to
taste

This is a south Indian style of dal called Toor Dal. Think of thick lentil soup with a smoky after-kick. Indians typically serve it with white rice, but I'm recommending against that here. If you can't help yourself, though, make sure the ratio of dal to rice on your plate is three to one.

**SERVES 4 AS A MAIN OR
6 AS A STARTER**

Pick over lentils (toss any discolored), and wash in several changes of cold water. Drain.

Purée tomatoes or dice them into small pieces. Place lentils in a large saucepan, add 5 cups of water, puréed tomatoes, turmeric, salt, and paprika. Bring to a boil over high heat for 5 minutes, then lower to medium and cook for 25 more minutes. Skim off surface froth and stir dal every 5 minutes. Cook until dal is thick and creamy. Turn off heat and let stand.

In a separate frying pan, heat cooking oil over medium heat until hot. Add fenugreek seeds; as soon as seeds start to brown lightly, add mustard seeds and immediately turn heat to low. (If you burned the fenugreek, discard and start over; they shouldn't be black.) As soon as mustard seeds start to pop, pour a cup of cooked dal into the frying pan. Cook on low for 5 minutes; return dal and seasoning to saucepan. Cook another 10 minutes, transfer to serving bowl, and serve. Add additional salt and pepper, to taste. The West Indian (Gujarati) variation includes sugar, to taste.

LENTILS

There's a reason lentils are the mainstay of diets throughout the world. Especially high in fiber, lentils are one of the most versatile legumes in the kitchen. They require no soaking and range from delicate pebbly French green lentils to the yellow-orange lentils used for making dal in Indian cookery. Pullman, Washington, has celebrated the National Lentil Festival every year since 1989; on the festival's website, I was reminded that Esau was tricked into selling his birthright for a pottage of lentils (Genesis 25:34). They really must have moved him...

BEETS

It took cooks a few hundred years to figure out that the root of the beet plant is as tasty as the leaves. Sadly, about two-thirds of the beetroot crop ends up in cans, which means most folks are eating soggy and metallic-tasting beets. No wonder I hated beets as a kid. The freshly cooked beet is another animal entirely. The Russians and Poles have figured this out. A peek in their refrigerators reveals shelves of pink foods (e.g., borscht, beet-dyed potato salad, coleslaw, macaroni, etc.). According to Culpeper, the famous English physician-herbalist of the seventeenth century, the beet "much loosens the belly, and is of a cleansing, digesting quality, and provokes urine." His beet revelations remain, for the most part, beyond dispute.

vegetarian borscht

This recipe comes from my dear Russian-born friend who swears by its efficacy. "We ate a lot of borscht and cabbage soup in my family, and honestly, I don't remember ever being constipated until I went to college. Is it soup in general that keeps you regular? Is it college in general that stops you up? I don't know." These are the sorts of questions that keep the Unconstipated Gourmet awake at night.

SERVES 4 AS A MAIN OR

6 AS A STARTER

I like to roast the beets a day ahead, so all my ingredients are ready to go when it's time to cook the soup. To prepare the beets, preheat oven to 400°F. Wash beets, cut into quarters, and place in an oven-proof skillet with 2 tablespoons of water, a dash of oil, and dashes of salt and pepper. Cover skillet with foil and roast beets for about an hour, until a fork easily pierces the flesh. Cool and peel.

When ready to make soup, place cabbage in a medium saucepot; add 4 cups of cold water or just enough to cover cabbage. Bring to a boil. Reduce heat to medium, and add salt, tomatoes, and potatoes. When potatoes are soft, after about 20 minutes, scoop them out of the pot with a slotted spoon; place

2-3 medium beets

2 tablespoons canola oil

4 cups fresh green cabbage, shredded

2 teaspoons salt

2-3 medium-size russet potatoes, peeled and halved

1 (15-ounce) can diced tomatoes

1 large carrot, cut into ¼-inch slices

1 large onion, chopped

1 teaspoon sugar

2 tablespoons ketchup

2 tablespoons fresh or dried dill

1-2 cloves garlic, minced

Salt and pepper, to taste

Sour cream

in a bowl and purée with an immersion blender, using a little water from the cabbage broth. Set mashed potatoes aside. Check cabbage. If already tender to taste, reduce heat to low. (You want to prevent excessive boiling.) Meanwhile, fry carrot in a small skillet with 1 tablespoon of oil until oil turns orange. Scrape into a bowl and set aside. In same pan, fry the onion, caramelizing it with the sugar, about 5–7 minutes.

Add the carrot, onion, and puréed potatoes back to the main pot of cabbage. Add ketchup. If cabbage is ready (it usually takes 20 to 25 min of cooking), turn off heat. Grate beets using a cheese grater and add to pot. Add the dill, garlic, and black pepper. Cover pot for 5 minutes, until the soup takes on a deep red color.

Serve hot, with a dollop of sour cream added to each bowl. A hearty whole-grain bread makes a good accompaniment, too.

caldo verde

This couldn't be easier to prepare, and it's one of those hearty, good-lookin' soups that you can serve as a main course at a dinner party with yummy bread and a salad; no one will think you're shirking your gourmet duties. And, although I have no scientific evidence to back me, I believe chorizo may be a laxative masquerading as a sausage.

1½ pounds kale or swiss chard

1½ pounds red potatoes, cubed

4 large garlic cloves, sliced

4-5 cups chicken stock

½ cup olive oil

8 ounces spicy chorizo, sliced thin

Salt and pepper, to taste

**SERVES 2 AS A MAIN OR
4 AS A STARTER**

Wash kale; strip leaves from stalk; chop leaves; discard stalks.

Place potatoes and garlic in large soup pot. Pour stock over and bring to a boil. Simmer until potatoes are soft. Without burning yourself, mash potatoes in broth. Add kale and sausage to soup. Simmer another 15 minutes. Season with salt and pepper.

KOREANS ON CONSTIPATION

A recent article in the *Korean Times* titled "Things We Should Know About Constipation" tested readers on their knowledge of the phenomenon. Among the true-false questions: Skipping breakfast causes constipation? Answer: True. Why? Because "putting food into the body can assist in getting the bowels to work," while "skipping meals can slow intestinal movement." But here's the question I liked best: "Women suffer more from constipation than men?" Answer: True. Women are twice as likely to complain of the ailment than men. Reasons: "Women eat less than men, which means they eat less fiber…and some women are reluctant to use public toilets, a factor which can increase their chances of getting constipated."

kimchi soup (a.k.a. kimchi chigae)

Health magazine listed kimchi in its top five "World's Healthiest Foods." It's rich in vitamins, aids digestion, and there's even speculation that it may retard cancers. If you didn't know this and just ate it, you might suspect, from the smoke coming out your ears, that it's gastrointestinally potent. Kimchi Chigae is a classic Korean soup made with kimchi. For this soup, Koreans prefer to use older kimchi that's developed more flavor, but use what you can get your hands on.

8 ounces bean sprouts

10 ounces firm tofu

2 cups spicy chopped kimchi (available at Asian markets or your local Korean restaurant)

2 (14½-ounce) cans chicken broth

1 cup water

3 green onions, chopped

Salt, to taste

1 cup leftover steak, brisket, bulgogi, or stew meat, thinly sliced (optional)

MAKES 6 STARTER SERVINGS

Clean sprouts. Cut tofu into cubes. In soup pot, combine kimchi, sprouts, tofu, chicken broth, and water. Cover and bring to a boil. Add green onions and salt (and meat, if you're so inclined). Bring back to a boil. Reduce to a simmer, and cook for 5 more minutes.

walnut garlic lentil soup

2 cups lentils

1 large onion, diced

1 bay leaf

4 tablespoons butter

6 cups stock (vegetable or chicken)

2-4 teaspoons salt

1-2 teaspoons pepper

4-6 garlic cloves (or more if you're a garlic person)

1 cup toasted walnuts

½ cup cream or half and half or crème fraîche

Parsley, minced

My neighbor, John, made this for us after our daughter was born and we were hard up for any nourishment— let alone nourishment that was friendly to the colon. He can't remember where he found the recipe, so if you're the inventor and want credit, I'm sorry, but I can't give it to you. Needless to say, you're a genius.

SERVES 4 AS A MAIN OR
6 AS A STARTER

Soak lentils for 2 hours. Drain. When lentils are done soaking, begin the soup. In a large soup pot, sauté onion and bay leaf in butter until translucent (you can caramelize a little to add sweetness). Add lentils, stock, and 1 teaspoon salt; bring to a boil, and then simmer for about 30 minutes. Meanwhile, using a mortar and pestle or any blunt object, mash garlic with a large pinch of salt. Add walnuts and mash to your desired consistency (I like it a little chunky, myself). Then add 2 tablespoons of the cream and desired amount of pepper. Add walnut-garlic paste to soup and mix. Pour in remaining cream. Taste. If you think the soup isn't garlicky enough, mash a bit more and add it to the main soup. Garnish each serving with parsley.

corn chowder

If you haven't read Anish Seth's foreword to this book, now's the time to go back and do so. Then make this soup. Then, the following day, brag about how light and airy you feel. It also happens to be a delicious soup...

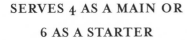

SERVES 4 AS A MAIN OR
6 AS A STARTER

Melt the butter in a large saucepan over medium heat. Add the bacon, salt pork, or ham. After a few minutes, the fat will start to pool. Turn off heat and pour out half the fat (into a compost bucket ideally, if your town allows animal fat in its compost... not down your drain). Return to medium heat and add the onion, carrot, and celery. Sauté for 4 minutes. Add the broth, potatoes, and bay leaf. Bring to a boil, cover, and turn heat to a simmer. When the potatoes are soft (about 15 minutes), add corn. Simmer another 2 minutes. Stir in milk and reheat thoroughly, but do not boil. Add salt and cayenne, to taste. Add thyme. Remove bay leaf. For a smoother consistency, this soup can be puréed (right before serving) with an immersion blender.

1 tablespoon butter

4 ounces of bacon or salt pork or ham, chopped roughly

½ cup chopped onion

⅓ cup chopped carrot

⅓ cup chopped celery

2½ cups chicken broth

1½ cup diced potato

1 bay leaf

1 cup whole milk

3 ears sweet corn, kernels removed, cobs discarded

½ teaspoon fresh thyme leaves

Salt and cayenne pepper, to taste

butternut squash soup

1 medium butternut squash

2½ tablespoons olive oil

1 cup chopped onion

¾ cup chopped carrot

¾ cup chopped celery

⅓ teaspoons nutmeg

¼ teaspoons dried thyme (or 1½ teaspoon fresh)

2 bay leaves

4 cups chicken stock

½ cup apple juice

Salt and pepper, to taste

"Butternut squash soup nips at the heels of chicken soup for world domination!" That'll be the 72-pt. headline running in newspapers in a few years. You heard it here first. It's sweeter, it's got more fiber, it's a tactile wonderland in the mouth, it's open to yummy garnishes like goat cheese and pumpkin seeds, and it's orange. I could just go on and on.

**SERVES 4 AS A MAIN OR
6 AS A STARTER**

Cut the squash in half, remove seeds, rub with ½ tablespoon olive oil, and sprinkle with salt. Roast in 400°F oven on a baking sheet for about 40 minutes or until soft. Allow to cool until you can touch it without burning your hands. Scoop out 2 cups of flesh. (Consider using the rest in a Squash Salad, page 109.) Set aside.

In a large soup pot, sauté onion in the remaining olive oil until soft. Add carrot and celery. After 5 minutes, add nutmeg, thyme, and bay leaves. Mix. Add chicken stock. When the soup boils, add apple juice. Return to a simmer. When the carrots are soft (about 20 minutes), add squash and turn off the heat. Remove bay leaves. With an immersion blender, purée the soup. Reheat. Add salt and pepper and serve. Particularly yummy with roasted and salted pumpkin seeds and a sprinkle of goat or feta cheese.

SQUASH

Ranging from tender summer varieties like zucchini and pattypans, to hearty winter butternuts and pumpkins, squash is rich in vitamins and full of soluble fiber. It's especially versatile in desserts, where high-fiber options are rare. Oh, and despite what you've heard, squash is a fruit, not a vegetable.

miso soup

⅛ cup dried wakame seaweed

6 cups broth made from dried bonito flakes (which the Japanese call dashi)

6½ cups water

1 ounce dried bonito flakes

¼ cup unpasteurized miso

½ lb soft tofu, drained and cut into ½-inch cubes

¼ cup thinly sliced scallion greens

Most Americans think of miso soup as an accompaniment to sushi, if they think of it at all. The Japanese often enjoy miso soup for breakfast. It's got the same fermented goodness as yogurt, plus it warms the belly, which can only be a good thing, especially if coffee is too potent for you. If you'd like to make this soup denser—more of a main dish than a side dish—consider adding clams, pumpkin, cabbage, and/or mushrooms to the water before adding the miso.

SERVES 4 AS A MAIN OR
6 AS A STARTER

Combine wakame seaweed with enough warm water to cover by 1 inch and let stand 15 minutes, or until reconstituted. Drain and rinse.

Meanwhile, put 6½ cups water in a large soup pot and heat to almost boiling. Just before the water boils, add bonito flakes. Let water boil. With a spoon, skim any foam off the top. Turn off the heat after 5 minutes. Strain the stock through a colander lined with a paper towel.

Stir together the miso and ½ cup dashi (bonito flake broth in a bowl until smooth. Reheat remaining dashi in its original pot (if you've let it cool) until hot, then stir in tofu and reconstituted wakame.

Simmer 1 minute and remove from heat. Immediately stir in miso mixture. Taste. Add more miso if you desire a stronger taste. Add scallions and serve.

TOOT YOUR OWN HORN

The Do-It-Yourself movement is in full swing. In the kitchen, do-it-yourselfers are making everything from homemade mustard to homemade miso. You can purchase miso starter culture online at gemcultures.com. Once it arrives, you start a little science experiment in the fridge involving miso spores, rice, and soybeans. Your family will love it—it's way better than nurturing a hamster. Note that the phrase *temae miso* ("homemade miso") means "to toot your own horn."

tortilla soup

2 tablespoons olive oil

½ cup chopped carrots

½ cup chopped celery

½ teaspoon salt

4 cups chicken stock

1½ cups chopped cooked
chicken (or turkey)

½ cup spicy salsa

1 avocado, sliced thin

½ cup shredded cheese
(something sharp, like
cheddar)

6 lime wedges

Thick tortilla chips, crushed

This is the soup I make the day after I roast a chicken or turkey. If it's cold outside, this soup makes me feel warm. If it's hot, this soup makes me feel like wearing a skirt and exposing my toes. Besides tasty meat, the key is in making or buying a very good, fresh salsa (do not use jarred salsa, if you can avoid it).

SERVES 2 AS A MAIN OR 4 AS A SIDE

This isn't cooking so much as warming up and decorating. You can certainly make the chicken stock from scratch, but if you're short on time, this version is plenty good. Heat up oil in large soup pot. Add the carrots, celery, and salt and lower heat to medium. After 5 minutes, add stock. Bring to a boil. Drop in chicken and turn heat to a simmer. Simmer for 15 minutes. Add salsa and simmer for another 5 minutes. Meanwhile, set out the toppings in small bowls: avocado, cheese, lime, and tortilla chips. Ladle the soup into bowls and serve. Tell your guests it requires all the toppings to be true tortilla soup. Serve with Coconut Cornbread (page 12) or Corn Cakes (page 10).

s a l a d s

Andy Raskin, author of *The Ramen King and I*, has become something of an expert on Japanese eating habits. He finds himself caught up with Japanese medical experts (and characters) like Dr. Hiromi Shinya, author of *Icho wa Kataru* (*The Digestive Tract Speaks*). The book is part memoir, part guide to intestinal self-help. In it, Dr. Shinya reflects on his early days as a physician in the United States. "When I looked at the intestines of Americans whose diet was primarily meat-based, I could hardly contain my astonishment. Their intestines were stiff and short…On the other hand, the intestines of people—even some Westerners—who subsisted entirely or primarily on a diet of grains, beans, vegetables, and fruits, tended to be very smooth and relatively long. The latter type is common among Japanese people, and leads to a much better intestinal condition."

couscous salad with cherry tomatoes and feta

For a long time, I was under the mistaken impression that couscous was difficult to prepare. Now, I impress friends with it all the time. The truth is that, on the difficulty scale, couscous is one step up from boiling water. On the Go-Meter, it's similarly well placed.

**SERVES 4–6 AS A SIDE,
WARM OR CHILLED**

Bring water to a boil, along with salt and pepper. Add the couscous, stir, cover, and turn off the heat. Let sit for 5 minutes, then uncover and toss with olive oil and lemon juice. Toast pine nuts on stovetop in small sauté pan. Stir every 2 minutes with wooden spoon, until lightly browned; on medium heat, it should take about 5 minutes. Add nuts to couscous.

In large bowl, prepare and mix remaining ingredients. Add couscous. Toss well.

2 cups water

½ teaspoon salt

Pinch freshly ground black pepper

1 cup whole-wheat couscous

3 tablespoons extra-virgin olive oil

2 tablespoons lemon juice

¼ cup pine nuts

⅓ cup chopped fresh basil

⅓ cup chopped shallot

1½ cups cherry tomatoes, chopped in halves

¾ cup crumbled feta cheese

OLIVE OIL

The Middle Eastern tradition of prophetic medicine has long held that olive oil keeps the internal machinery running smoothly. Prompted by the recent popularity of the olive-rich Mediterranean diet, researchers have confirmed that among its plethora of benefits, olive oil protects us from colorectal cancer. And what could possibly predispose a person to colorectal cancer? Constipation.

safsoof

This is essentially tabouli with chickpeas added, which means it's a mover with six cylinders instead of just four.

MAKES ENOUGH FOR 6 AS A SIDE

Cover and soak bulgur in warm water for 10 minutes. Drain through fine mesh strainer, pressing out water. Combine remaining salad ingredients. Combine dressing ingredients in small bowl, whisking oil, lemon juice, salt, pepper, and cayenne. Pour dressing over salad. Stir. Serve chilled.

½ cup medium bulgur

1 cup cooked chickpeas

3 medium tomatoes, chopped

1 small bunch green onions, chopped

½ cup mint, chopped fine

1 pickling cucumber, chopped

1 large bunch parsley, chopped

DRESSING:

¼ cup olive oil

¼ cup lemon juice

2 tablespoons balsamic vinegar

1 ½ teaspoons salt

½ teaspoon pepper

¼ teaspoon cayenne

all-american coleslaw

½ small green cabbage, shredded

½ small red cabbage, shredded

3 large carrots, grated

½ red onion, chopped

¼ cup parsley, minced

Salt and pepper, to taste

DRESSING:

1 cup canola oil

⅓ cup sugar

¾ cup apple cider vinegar

2 tablespoons Dijon mustard

Some might complain that this coleslaw lacks frills, but I would argue that the point of coleslaw is to act as a complement to other foods, not to steal the show. That's why I like my coleslaw "basic." There's no debating that any way you serve cabbage, it *works*.

MAKES ENOUGH FOR

10 SIDE SERVINGS

In a small saucepan, bring oil, sugar, and vinegar to a boil. Remove from heat and cool. Refrigerate. When chilled, add mustard and blend with whisk. In large bowl, mix all slaw ingredients. When ready to serve, pour dressing over. Toss and serve.

CABBAGE

The Irish get their cabbage in corned beef; the Americans in coleslaw; and the Russians in stuffed cabbage leaves and borscht. I could go on and on. Every country seems to have a cabbage staple. That's because the vegetable grows like a weed in most climates, stores well in winter, costs next to nothing, and is jammed with health properties (it's said to inhibit cancer, stimulate the immune system, kill harmful bacteria, sooth ulcers, and improve circulation, and that's on top of its un-constipating powers).

MANGA ON CONSTIPATION

According to Andy Raskin, my source for all things Japanese and food-related, there's yet more proof that the Japanese are actively and publicly engaged in debates about matters of regularity. A new manga series titled *Professor Genmai's Bento Box* stars one gut-obsessed academic who turns his Tokyo students on to traditional (slow) foods and organic farming. In Book 2, Episode 2, "The Body's Special Delivery," a few of the students become constipated; Professor Genmai lectures them on what makes an ideal b.m., and a guest lecturer leads them in "constipation calisthenics." In Episode 3, in conjunction with a doctor friend, Professor Genmai recommends a diet rich in fermented foods (rice bran pickles, yogurt, kimchi, etc.).

cucumber and pickled-plum salad

The Japanese swear by the miraculous umeboshi, or pickled plum. I found a website that recommends one umeboshi with some green tea every morning for regularity. That makes it the All-Bran of Japanese breakfasts. You can find umeboshi at specialty grocery stores like Whole Foods; the same goes for the cucumbers.

4 teaspoons umeboshi paste
(or you can finely chop
whole umeboshi)
4 teaspoons mirin
¼ cup chopped scallions
¼ cup chopped parsley
1½ cups chopped pickling or
Asian cucumbers

SERVES 2 AS A SIDE SALAD

In medium bowl, mix together the paste, mirin, scallions, and parsley. Add the cucumbers and coat with the paste mix. Serve immediately.

PROBING PROBIOTICS

If you've been living in a cave and just emerged, you might've missed the arrival of the term *probiotic* in the food news. Probiotic (as opposed to *antibiotic*) refers to the healthy bacteria often found in fermented foods like yogurt, kimchi, sauerkraut, etc. Probiotic zealots swear the presence of these bacteria in our guts makes us happier and healthier; they say that the more probiotic-rich food we eat, the better. Lately, I've heard it called a probiotic *movement*, which I find humorous, since movement is what probiotics also claim to achieve. There are now probiotic pills, granola bars, and specialty drinks. With all these new products comes controversy. Some say probiotic-rich foods must be refrigerated at all times or the good bacteria die before they can reach our guts. Others say sugar nullifies their effect, so yogurt with sweeteners, for instance, wouldn't have the same potency as yogurt without. It's hard to get a straight answer on all this. Golden rule on all fads: If you try it out, go for the least processed version of whatever's being pushed.

seaweed salad

This is an adaptation of Sandor Ellix Katz's special recipe. Katz is an expert on seaweed and all things fermented. He says, "Nothing nourishes the mucous membranes of the digestive tract and gets it moving better than seaweed." Needless to say, he was very supportive of this book and not only donated this recipe but a whole lesson on how to ferment food, why to ferment food, and what kind of vessel to ferment in. I couldn't fit his whole lesson here, but you can read more about it in his book *Wild Fermentation: The Flavor, Nutrition, and Craft of Live-Culture Foods,* or reach him at www.wildfermentation.com.

½ cup dried arame sea
   vegetables (seaweed)
2 tablespoons dark sesame oil
1 tablespoon minced ginger
1 bunch kale
1 tablespoon minced garlic
1½ tablespoons soy sauce (or
   more, if you like)
1 tablespoon red miso
1 tablespoon rice vinegar
1 tablespoon toasted sesame
   seeds
½ cup grated radishes
½ cup grated carrot

SERVES 4 AS A SIDE

Soak seaweed in water for 10 minutes. Drain and pour into a large mixing bowl. Add 1 teaspoon of dark sesame oil and the minced ginger.

Clean kale, separating the leaves from the stalks. Toss stalks. Chop leaves roughly. Set aside to drain a little.

Heat 2 teaspoons of dark sesame oil in a sauté pan. Add garlic for 45 seconds, and then add seaweed-ginger mix. Cook for another minute. Pour ingredients into a heat-resistant bowl and return sauté pan to burner. Add 1 tablespoon sesame oil to pan. Add chopped kale. Add 1 teaspoon soy sauce.

Using tongs, move kale around until coated with soy sauce. Cover; lower heat and let wilt, about 8 minutes, uncovering at end to evaporate some of the liquid. Pour kale into bowl with seaweed-ginger mixture. Add more sesame oil and soy sauce, to taste. Mix 1 tablespoon miso with 1 tablespoon rice vinegar, and incorporate mix into main salad. Let salad sit for 20 minutes or more on counter to cool. Add toasted sesame seeds, grated radishes, and carrots. Toss and serve.

asian coleslaw

Despite what I said about basic coleslaw, there *is* a place at the table for more complicated versions. It feels like impertinence NOT to share one with you.

SERVES 8 AS A SIDE

In a large bowl, mix the cabbages, carrots, and onions. Cover and refrigerate until 30 minutes before you're ready to serve. You can prepare your dressing in advance, too. Just whisk together all ingredients, then cover and refrigerate until you're ready to serve. Add dressing, a little bit at a time, until slaw is coated. (If you have extra dressing, save it for drizzling over a main course, salad, or rice noodles.) Garnish with roasted unsalted peanuts or sesame seeds, and cilantro. Eat within 1 hour of tossing with the dressing, or cabbage will wilt. (Note: Kept separate, the slaw and dressing will last a week in the refrigerator.)

3 cups thinly sliced green
cabbage

3 cups thinly sliced red cabbage

2 medium carrots, peeled,
cut into matchstick-size
strips or grated

8 green onions, chopped

DRESSING:

¼ cup soy sauce

¼ cup lemon juice

¼ cup canola oil

2 tablespoons grated
fresh ginger

2 tablespoons white vinegar

2 tablespoons dark brown sugar

2 teaspoons Asian sesame oil

1 teaspoon salt (or more,
to taste)

1 teaspoon black pepper

GARNISH:

1 cup roasted unsalted peanuts
(or 2 teaspoons sesame seeds)

½ cup chopped fresh cilantro

radishes and avocado
with miso-ginger dressing

8 radishes

1 avocado

DRESSING:

2 tablespoons red miso

2 teaspoons Dijon mustard

1 tablespoon water

1½ tablespoons fresh
  lemon juice

¼ cup olive or vegetable oil

1 teaspoon peeled and
  minced ginger

1 scallion, minced

A friend tried this and declared it her new summer salad standard. It helps that one batch of the dressing will probably last you an entire season. It packs a flavor wallop, so you only need the tiniest of drizzles on the plate.

MAKES 2 SMALL SIDE SALADS

(BUT ENOUGH DRESSING FOR ABOUT 8)

To prepare dressing, mash together miso and mustard in a medium bowl; add water and lemon juice. Blend. Pour in oil in a steady stream, whisking until emulsified. Add gingerroot and scallion. Blend. Set aside.

Slice radishes into rounds. Slice avocado into neat slices. Arrange on 2 plates. Drizzle dressing over, and serve.

MISO

A savory, spicy soup base and seasoning, miso is made by inoculating soybeans with a special mold and letting the mix ferment for several months. Naturally fermented, raw miso is rich in potent enzymes that break hard-to-digest carbohydrates into simple sugars. This makes the fiber-rich soybeans super-easy to digest. Miso also delivers a load of friendly probiotic bacteria to the gut, where they set up colonies and continue digesting for us. Miso comes in several colors and flavors. White miso tends to be sweeter (and is actually yellow), and red miso is saltier (and actually brown); there's a blended version too, which splits the difference.

cold soba salad with garlic and peanuts

8 ounces buckwheat soba noodles

1 cup cucumber rounds

½ cup unsalted, roasted peanuts

DRESSING:

½ cup chopped scallion

2 large garlic cloves

3 tablespoons tamari soy sauce

3 tablespoons chopped cilantro

2 tablespoons sesame paste or peanut butter

2 tablespoons rice wine

1½ tablespoons rice vinegar

1 tablespoon dark sesame oil

1 tablespoon honey

½ teaspoon Chinese chili paste

Pinch five-spice powder

Make sure to find soba noodles with fiber in them, as there are several manufacturers out there, and some get away with watered-down fiber content (look for 100 percent buckwheat, ideally). Also, the garlic here is not for the faint-hearted.

SERVES 2 AS A LIGHT LUNCH OR SIDE

In a blender, purée dressing ingredients until smooth. Cook the soba noodles according to package directions. While still warm (but after draining), toss into a bowl with dressing. Mix well. Serve at room temperature with peanuts and cucumbers on top.

cucumbers, tomatoes, and red cabbage with tahini dressing

One of the gastroenterologists I interviewed for this book had a lot of things to say about lettuce. His patients are always coming to him and saying, "Doctor, I don't get it. I eat a salad every day and I'm still constipated." The doctor shakes his head at these patients and asks knowingly, "What's in these salads of yours?" The patients reply: "Lettuce." Aha! "Lettuce is your problem," the doctor informs them. "Exchange the lettuce for spinach or chopped vegetables and you will see a substantial difference in your regularity." And they do. Unfortunately, the gastroenterologist has no evidence to prove that lettuce is constipating his patients. Twenty-five years of observation has given him a strong hunch, however... Here, just to be safe, the cukes, tomatoes, and cabbage will be filling in for lettuce.

1½ cups pickling cucumbers, chopped

1 cup cherry tomatoes, halved

1 cup chopped red cabbage

DRESSING:

1 cup tahini

¾ cup canola oil

¼ cup olive oil

¼ cup red wine vinegar

¼ cup lemon juice

5 garlic cloves, chopped

1 teaspoon salt

⅓ teaspoon cayenne

¼ teaspoon cumin

1 cup water

SERVES 4 AS A SIDE

Blend all dressing ingredients, except for the water, in a food processor. Add water slowly. Dressing should be smooth and creamy. Don't add more water than you need (i.e., avoid making a soup). Refrigerate. Dressing should keep for 2 weeks in a sealed container. When ready to serve, bring to room temperature and drizzle over plated salad vegetables. Salad is doubly good with fresh cucumber, radishes, and feta cheese.

jerusalem artichoke salad with bacon

6 Jerusalem artichokes, washed, trimmed, peeled, and sliced into inch-thick chunks

4 slices bacon

2 shallots, chopped fine

3 tablespoons balsamic vinegar (preferably a good white balsamic)

1 tablespoon French mustard

Extra-virgin olive oil, to taste

1 small handful flat parsley, chopped

½ cup toasted walnut halves

1 bag of mixed lettuces

Salt and pepper, to taste

Parmesan cheese, shaved (optional)

These artichokes, which aren't really artichokes, have an interesting reputation. They're probably best known for causing gas. That's because they're often under-cooked, and an undercooked Jerusalem artichoke WILL provoke toots. So, to be safe, overcook the first time and serve to your nearest and dearest only.

SERVES 4 AS A SIDE

Preheat oven to 425°F. Roast Jerusalem artichoke chunks on baking sheet until soft and brown, about 20 minutes. Sauté bacon in small skillet, until crisp and brown. Drain on paper towels. Wipe skillet, leaving a remnant of bacon fat for cooking shallots. Sauté shallots for 2 minutes until slightly wilted. Turn off heat. Add the vinegar, mustard, olive oil, and parsley. Stir. In large wooden serving bowl, toss lettuce with warm Jerusalem artichokes, walnuts, bacon, and shallot dressing. Serve with shaved Parmesan cheese.

JERUSALEM ARTICHOKES

Also called sunchokes, Jerusalem artichokes are not actually artichokes, and not really connected with the city of Jerusalem. Native to North America, they were cultivated from Maine to Texas long before Europeans invented those states. They contain inulin, a "prebiotic," or feast-for-the-gut bacteria. If your gut flora aren't very strong, inulin can be difficult to digest, producing what the seventeenth-century English botanist, John Goodyer, called "a filthy loathsome stinking wind within the body." Inulin, fortunately, breaks down with sufficient cooking.

persimmon goat cheese salad with pumpkin seeds

¾ cup pumpkin seeds

½ teaspoon salt

½ tablespoon olive oil

3 ounces soft goat cheese

Freshly ground pepper, to taste

10 cups mixed greens

2 fuyu persimmons, peeled and
   cut into wedges

1 pomegranate, seeded

DRESSING:

½ cup pomegranate juice

2 tablespoons walnut or extra-
   virgin olive oil

2 teaspoons honey

1 garlic clove, finely minced

This salad has lots of textures and is perfect with lamb or brisket on a cold night. One can imagine the ancient Greeks eating this for dinner and prostrating to the gods the following morning.

SERVES 6

Preheat oven to 400°F. Toss the pumpkin seeds with ½ tablespoon olive oil, followed by ½ teaspoon salt, and spread them on a baking sheet. Roast for 10 minutes, watching closely to avoid scorching. Remove from oven when nicely colored and aromatic. Spread on a dinner plate and let cool for about 10 minutes. Leave the oven on. Meanwhile, mix dressing ingredients (to encourage the honey to blend with other ingredients, you may need to heat the dressing in a microwave for about 20 seconds). Heap salad greens on individual plates. Decorate with persimmon wedges and pomegranate seeds. Pinch off pieces of goat cheese to form 1-inch rounds. Sprinkle with pepper and roll in cooled pumpkin seeds. Place goat cheese rounds on same baking sheet you used for pumpkin seeds. Heat for about 3 minutes in oven. Drizzle dressing over salads. Top each with goat cheese.

PUMPKIN SEEDS

Next time Halloween comes around, carve the pumpkin and SAVE the seeds. Traditionally hulled, soaked in brine, and dried or roasted, pumpkin seeds ("pepitas" in Spanish) are popular in Mexican cookery and are used as a laxative in Ethiopia. They're also known to purge parasites and fill in for oysters as an aphrodisiac…in a pinch.

PEARS

Of pears, Culpeper, the famous English physician-herbalist of the seventeenth century, writes: "…All the sweet and luscious sorts, whether manured or wild, do help to move the belly downwards, more or less. Those that are hard and sour, do, on the contrary, bind the belly as much, and the leaves do so also." His ancient assessment coupled with what we know now—pears are fiber bowling balls—make this fruit an excellent grab when walking out the door for a sedentary afternoon at the office.

pear, blue cheese, and avocado salad with walnuts

This salad is the leafy-green embodiment of California. As if the pear doesn't have enough going for it—gutwise—there's avocado and blue cheese to make it go down smoother.

SERVES 4 AS A SIDE

Wash lettuce and arrange on 4 plates. Decorate each mound of lettuce with the pears, avocados, onions, a sprinkling of blue cheese, and walnuts. Whisk together all dressing ingredients, and spoon over each salad.

1 head of romaine or 4 cups of mixed lettuces

1 ½ ripe pears, cut into slices

1 ½ avocados, peeled and cut into slices

¼ red onion, sliced

4 ounces blue or gorgonzola cheese, crumbled

1 cup toasted walnuts

DRESSING:

½ cup olive oil

¼ cup sherry vinegar

1 tablespoon Dijon mustard

1 teaspoon fresh thyme

Salt and pepper, to taste

green papaya salad

2 cups fresh, green (unripe)
papaya

½ pound green beans, ends
removed

1½ cups shredded red cabbage

½ cup chopped cilantro

½ cup crushed peanuts

DRESSING:

3-4 large cloves garlic

4-6 fresh Thai chilies
(or whatever hot chilies
you can find), chopped

2 tablespoons fish sauce

2 tablespoons fresh lime juice

1½ tablespoons sugar

This is a staple of Thai and Laotian diets, and is it any wonder why? Papaya is God's gift to the gut. Eat this salad with barbecued chicken and sticky rice (but not too much rice, or you'll offset the papaya's magic).

SERVES 4 AS A SIDE

Boil 3 cups of water in a small saucepan. Prepare an ice bath in a medium-sized bowl. While the water is heating, peel the papaya and rinse with running water. Discard seeds. Shred papaya meat with the finest setting on a cheese grater. Set aside. Drop green beans into boiling water and cook for about 2 minutes, until no longer woody to taste. Immediately drain beans and drop in ice bath to preserve their color. Place garlic cloves and chilies in a mortar, and mash with a pestle until well blended and chunky (you can use a fork or blender for this, too). Add the fish sauce, lime juice, and sugar, and blend again. Arrange the cabbage on a platter. Top with cooled green beans and shredded papaya. Pour dressing over. Sprinkle with the cilantro and nuts before serving. Serve cold.

beet and pomegranate salad

Any beet will work in this salad, but I like golden for diversity of color. Also, if you can get your hands on a well-made white balsamic vinegar (instead of the cheap, acrid red kind), do it; it's hard to find but much lighter and sweeter than standard balsamic. Finally, this is an autumn dish, as you won't find pomegranate in the middle of summer.

SERVES 4 AS A SIDE

Preheat oven to 400°F. Whisk dressing ingredients together. Add diced onion to the dressing now, if you prefer a less potent onion flavor. To roast beets, first rinse, cut into quarters, and place in an oven-proof sauté pan. Add water, orange juice, olive oil, and dashes of salt and pepper. Cover with foil and roast for 1 hour. Let cool until you can touch them without steam-burning yourself, and then peel and slice into wedges (dispose of orange juice-olive oil mixture). Wash and dry lettuce and arrange on plates. Place beet wedges in overlapping layers atop the lettuce. Sprinkle with pomegranate seeds and feta (and onion, if you haven't already added it to the dressing). Drizzle dressing over salad, as desired.

3 large beets (preferably golden)

2 tablespoons orange juice

1½ tablespoons olive oil

½ cup diced red onion

½ cup pomegranate seeds

2 cups mixed lettuces

¼ cup crumbled feta cheese

DRESSING:

½ cup olive oil

¼ cup balsamic vinegar

1 tablespoon Dijon mustard

1 teaspoon fresh thyme

Salt and pepper, to taste

gorgonzola-stuffed dried fig salad

½ red onion

½ cup balsamic vinegar

12 large dried figs, stems removed

4 ounces gorgonzola cheese

1 bag or head of lettuce (butter or mixed spring greens)

¾ cup olive oil

1 teaspoon Dijon mustard

Salt and pepper, to taste

I first came across a version of this recipe when I was 13 years old. It was printed on the back of a pack of Calimyrna dried figs. The packager was clearly pushing figs as more than just an afternoon snack. And they ARE more than that. I've since doctored the recipe so it's got more *brio*. I like to save it for those moments when last-minute guests show up, expecting culinary pyrotechnics in short order.

SERVES 4 AS A SIDE

Cut the onion into rings. In a glass bowl (with a cover), soak rings in the balsamic vinegar. Let sit covered for 10 to 15 minutes while preparing remainder of salad. With your finger, press a hole into the top of each dried fig (where the stem was). Break off a pinch of cheese (about a half-inch square) and stuff into the hole. Place all 12 stuffed figs onto a tray and heat in the toaster or oven—at 350°F—for 7 to 10 minutes, until the cheese begins to ooze. While the figs are cooking, wash and dry your lettuce and arrange equal portions on 4 plates. Add olive oil, mustard, salt, and pepper to balsamic-onion mixture. Cover and shake until well blended. When figs are done heating, arrange 3 on each mound of greens. Pour a dash of dressing over each plate and serve while the figs are still warm.

CHEESE WITH BUTTER, PLEASE

I'm particularly fond of this 150-year-old advice regarding cheese. "Cut a pound of good, rich cheese into bits, add to it two ounces of fresh butter, and rub them together in a mortar till quite smooth. This is an excellent way of eating cheese for dyspeptics. Spread it on bread, and it is very good." This is also a recipe for a heart attack, but whatever. The pounding is also curious. Does smoothing the mixture out make it more digestible? Too bad the author isn't around to ask.

Anna Maria Collins, The Great Western Cook Book, or Table Receipts,
Adapted to Western Housewifery, (A. S. Barnes & Company, New York) 1857

black bean and roasted corn salad with mango

1 tablespoon canola oil

2 garlic cloves, minced

3 cups fresh corn kernels, cut
   from the cob (about 4 ears)

2 cups diced mango

2 (15-ounce) cans black beans,
   rinsed and drained

1 cup chopped red onion

⅓ cup fresh lime juice

3 tablespoons chopped cilantro

½ teaspoon salt

½ teaspoon ground cumin

1 chipotle pepper in adobo
   sauce, chopped fine (available
   in cans)

8 cups salad greens

A perfect salad for Independence Day...regular on the Fourth of July.

SERVES 6 AS A SIDE

Heat oil in a cast-iron skillet. Add garlic; let sizzle for 30 seconds, then quickly add corn. Sear corn for about 10 minutes, tossing every few minutes until well browned. Pour warm, cooked corn into a bowl; add mango and remaining ingredients, except the lettuce. Toss. Serve on individual plates, first laying down a mound of greens and then a scoop of salad.

BLACK BEANS

Like all legumes, black beans are high in fiber and protein, along with a goodly dose of minerals like iron. They also contain loads of molybdenum (best word from high school chemistry), which helps detoxify sulfites, those chemicals in wine and dried fruit that give you headaches. In addition to insoluble fiber, they have the highest concentration of soluble fiber of anything grown under the sun (close second: oat bran). Soluble fiber doesn't just absorb water and shoot on out, like insoluble fiber; instead, it ferments in your gut, producing healthy byproducts and feeding the friendly bacteria. And because black beans are so dark in color, they are as full of antioxidants as grapes and cranberries.

red lentil salad

3 cups red lentils

6 cups water

5 tablespoons olive oil

4 tablespoons red wine vinegar

3 large cloves garlic,

    finely minced

1½ teaspoons salt

¼ teaspoon black pepper

2 tablespoons fresh oregano,

    finely chopped (or about

    1 tablespoon dried)

2 stalks celery, diced

½ cup crumbled feta cheese

    (optional)

1 cup cherry tomatoes, halved

    (optional)

For me, this is just intuitive "regular" food. The Greeks, the Indians, and all the other lentil-loving people of the world are on to something. We should follow their lead.

SERVES 6 AS A SIDE

Rinse lentils and toss out water. Bring lentils and water to a boil in a medium pot. Cook until soft but firm (10 minutes plus; don't let them get mushy). Meanwhile, dice the celery. Whisk olive oil and vinegar in a small bowl; add garlic, salt, pepper, oregano, and celery. Once the lentils are done, drain and rinse. Toss with the dressing and, if you choose, the feta and tomatoes.

succotash salad

Summer, summer, summer. Many report that they're more regular in the summer than in the winter. But in case you're not one of those lucky few, here's a summer recipe that's sure to help.

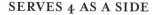

SERVES 4 AS A SIDE

Boil corn for 3 minutes. Let sit and cool. If using frozen edamame, follow directions to cook through. If using precooked, shell 2 cups and place in a bowl with tomatoes and basil. Cut cooled corn from cob and add to salad. In separate bowl, mix lime juice or vinegar, olive oil, mustard, salt, and pepper. Pour dressing over salad and toss.

4 ears sweet corn, yellow or white

2 cups packaged, precooked, or frozen raw edamame (lima beans work, too)

1 cup cherry tomatoes, halved

½ cup basil, chopped

3 tablespoons lime juice or white balsamic vinegar

4 tablespoons olive oil

1 teaspoon Dijon mustard

Salt and pepper, to taste

IF OPRAH SAYS SO, IT MUST BE TRUE

Oprah Winfrey recently lit up the constipation switch-board when she invited her über-popular medical expert, Dr. Oz, to talk about it to her faithful minions. He used a phrase I'd never heard before, "safe-toilet syndrome." It refers, he said, to the habit we humans have of not relaxing when faced with a foreign potty; the not-relaxing leads to not taking care of business. So no matter how many bran muffins you eat at the hotel's continental breakfast, and no matter how many cups of coffee you may drink, you may still strike out while on vacation.

roasted butternut squash, radicchio, and feta salad

I served this at a dinner party once, and from the amazed reactions, you'd think I'd planted and harvested the squash myself. In fact, this salad is fairly easy. The squash can be roasted a day in advance; all the other ingredients can be put together an hour before serving. It's beautiful to look at, but once it reaches the gut, who cares.

SERVES 4 TO 6 AS A SIDE

Preheat oven to 400°F. On a large baking sheet, toss squash with olive oil and salt. Roast until tender, about 40 minutes. Move to top rack and broil for 2 minutes until browned. Cool and refrigerate for at least 1 hour (and up to a day). Meanwhile, whisk together dressing ingredients and let sit at least 1 hour.

Place cooled squash, salad greens, feta, onion, and pine nuts in a salad bowl. Toss with dressing and salt.

1 butternut squash, peeled, seeded, and cut into 2-inch cubes

1 tablespoon olive oil

1 teaspoon salt

2 cups mixed greens

8 ounces feta, crumbled

1 small red onion, chopped

⅓ cup toasted pine nuts

DRESSING:

Juice of 2 limes

2 tablespoons peanut oil

1 tablespoon Dijon mustard

½ teaspoon salt

¼ teaspoon olive oil

Salt and pepper, to taste

roasted winter squash with chopped cabbage and miso

1 pound winter squash

1 tablespoon sesame oil, for roasting

3 cups shredded cabbage (any kind)

1 tablespoon toasted sesame seeds

DRESSING:

¼ cup white miso (low-salt, if you can find it)

2 tablespoons unsalted rice vinegar

1½ tablespoons peanut oil

1 tablespoon sesame oil

1 tablespoon sesame paste

1 teaspoon soy sauce

1 teaspoon minced ginger

1 teaspoon honey (or more, to taste)

1 clove minced garlic

An alternative salad to accompany the Thanksgiving turkey and prevent the after-dinner blahs.

SERVES 4 AS A SIDE

Preheat oven to 450°F. Use an electric blender with a sharp blade to purée the dressing ingredients. Set aside. Remove squash skin with paring knife, discard seeds, and cut into 1½-inch chunks. Toss in 1 table-spoon sesame oil. Roast for 10 to 15 minutes, turning once, until soft. Then move up to broiler rack and broil for 1 to 2 minutes, turning once. Squash should be nicely browned. Remove from oven. Toss cabbage with dressing (you won't need all of it, and once it's on the cabbage, it needs to be eaten within 1 hour or the cabbage will wilt). Arrange cabbage mounds on 4 plates. Add about ½ cup squash to each mound and sprinkle with sesame seeds (which you can "toast" or brown quickly in a frying pan, tossing frequently). The salad can be eaten warm or cold.

SESAME SEEDS

On top of their high nutrient count (copper, iron, zinc, calcium), sesame seeds also contain two special kinds of fiber—sesamin and sesamolin, which are lignans that lower cholesterol, prevent high blood pressure, protect the liver, stave off cancer, and feed healthy bacteria in your gut. In traditional Chinese medicine, sesame seeds are used to "moisten dryness," which I am told means "treat constipation." The traditional medium for this treatment is a milk-like soup made from black sesame seeds and rice. Sesame seeds are also delicious mashed up as tahini, the paste used in hummus and candies like halvah. And of course, sesame seeds are magic…"Open sesame."

sides

"A savoury pie for persons of delicate digestion. Cut up fowl and sweetbread, lay in the dish in alternate layers with meat, jelly, and the yolks of hard-boiled eggs without the whites, and flavor with lemon-juice, white pepper, and salt; cover with rice prepared as follows: boil half a pound of rice in sufficient water to permit it to swell; when tender beat it up to a thick paste with the yolk of one or two eggs, season with a little salt, and spread it over the dish thickly. The fowl and sweetbread should have been previously simmered till half done in a little weak broth; the pie must be baked in a gentle oven, and if the rice will not brown sufficiently, finish with a salamander."

Judith Cohen Montefiore, The Jewish Manual of Practical Information in Jewish and Modern Cookery with a Collection of Valuable Recipes & Hints Relating to the Toilette 1846

chard with miso and sesame

When you grow tired of sautéing your greens in garlic and olive oil, try this Asian twist, which gets a bonus GI boost from sesame seeds.

SERVES 4 AS A SIDE

Boil 6 cups of salted water in a large pot. Place clean chard leaves in a small colander (that fits into pot). Dunk colander with chard into boiling water and keep leaves submerged for a few seconds, until leaves turn a brighter green and begin to look limp. Remove from heat and run cold water over chard. When cool to the touch, squeeze liquid from chard.

In large bowl, mix sesame paste, miso, soy sauce, and vinegar until thick and smooth. Toss chard with a few spoonfuls of sauce. Taste. Add more sauce if necessary. Add tofu and sesame seeds. Toss again, gently.

1 bunch chard, cleaned, stems removed, and shredded (or substitute dino kale or spinach)

1 tablespoon Japanese sesame paste

1½ tablespoons white miso

½ teaspoon soy sauce

2 tablespoons rice vinegar

¼ cup crumbled firm tofu

1 teaspoon toasted sesame seeds, toasted

SWISS CHARD

Called a "vegetable valedictorian" by the World's Healthiest Foods website, chard clocks in with 716 percent of your daily recommended vitamin K. It also has everything else, from folate to fiber. Aristotle recognized its value in 350 BC. Today, slightly more advanced studies have shown that chard's phytonutrients and fiber make it particularly effective in preventing digestive-tract cancers. Swiss chard goes by a couple different names, including white beet, strawberry spinach, seakale beet, leaf beet, Sicilian beet, spinach beet, Chilean beet, Roman kale, and silverbeet.

sautéed chard
with garlic

The French have been tossing around theories about constipation for centuries. These days, Swiss chard is believed to be the magic bullet, according to my American friend living in Provençe. This is perhaps the easiest and tastiest way to whip it into action.

2 bunches Swiss chard
(rainbow or green)

2 tablespoons olive oil

4 large garlic cloves,
thinly sliced

1 teaspoon salt

Juice of half a lemon (optional)

SERVES 4 AS A SIDE

Strip chard leaves from stalks. Wash both. Chop stalks into thin slivers. Chop leaves coarsely. Heat large skillet. Add oil. Add garlic. Sauté for 30 seconds on medium heat. Add ½ cup of chopped stalks. Sauté for 2 minutes. Add a dash of salt. Toss. Add chard leaves. Toss so all leaves wilt. Add remainder of salt. Sauté until leaves are tender, but still bright green. Optional: Sprinkle with lemon juice before serving.

brussels sprouts with bacon and shallots

4 slices uncured bacon

1 tablespoon olive oil

½ cup shallots, minced

1½ pounds Brussels sprouts, halved

1 cup chicken broth

Salt and pepper, to taste

Brussels sprouts are my favorite vegetable. This has much to do with their regular pairing with bacon. Their efficacy is incidental...

SERVES 4 TO 6 AS A SIDE

In a cast-iron skillet or large sauté pan, brown bacon strips. Drain browned bacon on paper towels and pour off 95 percent of the fat. When bacon is cool, use your fingers to crumble it; place in medium bowl. Set aside. Sauté shallots for 3 minutes in remaining fat. Scrape from pan into bowl with bacon. Set aside. Add olive oil to pan, and turn flame to high. Add Brussels sprouts. Sprinkle 1 teaspoon salt over sprouts. Don't stir for 2 to 3 minutes, so sprouts get nice and brown on 1 side. Then, shake pan to turn sprouts. Cook for another 3 minutes on high. Add broth. Bring to a boil, then simmer, covered, for 8 to 10 minutes, until the sprouts are tender and most of the broth is absorbed. Stir bacon and shallots back into skillet. Add salt and pepper.

BRUSSELS SPROUTS

Another A+ member of the cabbage family, Brussels sprouts have achieved status recently as cooks realize they needn't actually be cooked to a homogenous mush. They're ridiculously nutritious and—for our purposes— high in fiber and other colon-friendly nutrients, from omega-3s to tryptophan.

PLUMS ARE LIKE WOMEN

"All Plums are under Venus, and are like women, some better, and some worse. As there is great diversity of kinds, so there is in the operation of Plums, for some that are sweet moistens the stomach, and make the belly soluble; those that are sour quench thirst more, and bind the belly; the moist and waterish do sooner corrupt in the stomach, but the firm do nourish more, and offend less. The dried fruit sold by the grocers under the names of Damask Prunes do somewhat loosen the belly, and being stewed, are often used, both in health and sickness, to relish the mouth and stomach, to procure appetite, and a little to open the body, allay choler, and cool the stomach."

Nicholas Culpeper, Culpeper's Complete Herbal *1652*

tzimmes

This dish, a Jewish staple, means "big fuss" in Yiddish. Perhaps it was a big fuss to make back in the days before electric mixers, but it's hardly a fuss now. Make it a day in advance to let the flavors meld. Serve with a hearty meat like brisket or pot roast. If it's too sweet, cut down on the honey or nix it altogether. It makes a ton, so invite a crowd. The baby of the house may enjoy this too (it's perfect for the toothless).

SERVES 6 AS A SIDE

In a soup pot, sauté onion in butter over medium heat. When soft, about 5 minutes, add carrots, sweet potatoes, prunes, apricots, honey, zest, juice, cinnamon, nutmeg, and salt. When it bubbles, lower the heat to a simmer. Cover. Cook until potatoes are soft, about 1 hour. Stir occasionally. Turn off heat. Using an immersion blender, mix tzimmes until it's a mashed potato consistency. Cover and keep warm. Meanwhile, roast walnuts in pan or in oven (at 400°F) until brown and aromatic (about 7 minutes). Add pepper and more salt to tzimmes if needed. Toss again, then turn tzimmes onto a platter and sprinkle with walnuts. Note: Some prefer tzimmes chunky; if that's you, forgo the immersion blender step.

1 large yellow onion, finely chopped

2 tablespoons butter

1 pound carrots, sliced like coins

1 pound sweet potatoes, peeled and cut into small pieces

4 ounces pitted, unsulfured prunes

4 ounces chopped, dried, unsulfured apricots

3 tablespoons honey

Zest of 1 orange and 1 lemon

Juice of 2 oranges and 2 lemons

½ teaspoon ground cinnamon

½ teaspoon nutmeg

1 teaspoon salt

½ teaspoon pepper

¾ cup roasted walnuts

steamed artichokes with aioli

½ cup mayonnaise

2 tablespoons chopped chives

2 tablespoons chopped parsley

2 tablespoons chopped dill

2 tablespoons capers

1 tablespoon olive oil

½ teaspoon Dijon mustard

Salt and pepper, to taste

4 large artichokes, outer leaves, base, and tips removed

When I was growing up, the hilt of sophistication was dipping a warm artichoke into a neon yellow mayonnaise-lemon-mustard concoction. That's all well and good for the '70s, but now we know better. For real taste, one must make the aioli sauce from scratch.

SERVES 6 AS AN APPETIZER OR SIDE

In a bowl with a tight-fitting lid, use a spoon to blend mayonnaise, chives, parsley, dill, capers, olive oil, and mustard. Season with salt and pepper. Cover and refrigerate for up to 24 hours.

To steam artichokes, boil a quarter inch of water in a pot fitted with a steamer rack. Make sure the water doesn't come up over the rack's bottom. When water boils, set artichokes on rack. Reduce heat to a slow boil. Cover and steam for about 50 minutes. You should be able to easily pierce the artichoke stems with a knife when the artichokes are done. Let cool for 10 minutes. Serve in a big bowl; scoop aioli into a ramekin and place beside artichokes. Put out a bowl for discarded skins as well.

elote

You can eat corn on the cob plain and get the same fiber kick, but this is a dressed-up version that everyone should try at least once. Bring extra napkins to the table, as well as corn grips, if you've got them. You may develop a cayenne-mayo mustache while eating, but so will the person across the table, so it all works out.

4 ears corn

3 tablespoons mayonnaise

2 tablespoons fresh lime juice

2 tablespoons finely grated
   Parmesan cheese

¼–½ teaspoon chili powder

¼ teaspoon ground cumin

⅛ teaspoon salt

Pinch of ground red pepper

SERVES 4 AS A SIDE

Boil a pot of salted water. Add corn and boil for 5 minutes. While it's cooking, combine mayo and lime juice on a dinner plate (you will be rolling the corn through this mix eventually). Combine the cheese and seasonings on another plate. When ears are ready, roll them through the mayo mix first, followed by the cheese mix. Serve hot (and with corn grips, if you have them—otherwise you'll be licking your fingers throughout the meal). Goes nicely with any traditional BBQ fare—ribs, chicken, burgers, hot dogs, steaks, etc. Incidentally, if you do happen to have a BBQ hot and ready to go when the corn is done boiling, pop the ears onto the grill for a minute or less to give them some tasty char, and then roll them in the toppings.

fresh corn tortillas

2 cups instant corn masa mix

2 teaspoons salt

1¼ cups warm water

There are some really bad corn tortillas tramping around grocery stores across America—dry, thin, and bland—and they give all corn tortillas a bad name. To give the corn tortilla back its good standing, you must make it from scratch and eat it warm. You'll love it coming and going.

MAKES 10-12 TORTILLAS

Blend together dry mix and salt in large mixing bowl. Stir in water to form a crumbly dough. Knead dough until smooth, about 4 minutes. Add water if dry. Cover with plastic wrap. Refrigerate for 30 minutes.

Remove from refrigerator. Pinch off golf-ball-sized portions. Roll dough with hands or rolling pin. If you want crispy tortillas, roll thin. If you want chewy, roll a little thicker. Place on a preheated griddle or cast-iron skillet. Cook about 1 minute per side. Check to make sure they've cooked through.

Stack cooked tortillas between cloth napkins to keep warm while preparing the remainder. Serve with guacamole, salsa, Black Bean Soup (page 60), or as a "bread" with salads.

CORNMEAL

Like other whole grains, cornmeal is high in fiber. It also has lots of folate and is very versatile in cooking, especially for people suspicious of whole grains. On the flip side, many folks just can't believe that grits, hominy, and polenta might actually be good for us.

braised red cabbage

4 cups red cabbage, shredded (outer leaves removed)

1 cup water

½ tart apple, chopped

1 tablespoon brown sugar

1 teaspoon salt

¼ teaspoon pepper

2 teaspoons flour

2 tablespoons cider vinegar

I first had this at my husband's favorite German restaurant, the Kaiserhof, in the tiny town of Bradford, Illinois. There's a reason why it's often paired with heavy German dishes like schnitzel or bratwursts. It chases them in and out.

SERVES 4 AS A SIDE

In a soup pot, combine cabbage and water. Bring to a boil, and then simmer until leaves wilt, about 5 minutes. Add the apple, sugar, salt, and pepper. You may need to add more water as well, if it's evaporating fast. Cover. Continue to simmer, stirring occasionally, for 10 minutes. Meanwhile, mix flour with 2 teaspoons water and vinegar in a small bowl. Add to cabbage. Stir. The stewing liquid should thicken after a few minutes. Serve hot.

LIFE IS LIKE A CHICKEN COOP LADDER…

I'd heard it rumored that Germans were a scatologically-obsessed people, but I didn't believe it until I found *Life Is Like a Chicken Coop Ladder, a Study of German National Character Through Folklore*, by the late Alan Dundes, an influential folklorist. Among Germans "there is…a literal daily concern with the act of defecation," according to Dundes. "A solicitous mother may address the following rhetorical question to her infant: 'Hast du die Hose voll (gemacht)?' [Have you (made) a pants full?] often accompanying the inquiry with a tender fact-finding pat on the buttocks…Many adult Germans ask themselves each morning, 'Werde ich heute Stuhlgang haben?' [Will I have a bowel movement today?] Family members may typically question one another on this matter at some length. Such frank discussions often shock or surprise American listeners unfamiliar with this facet of German culture. A traditional rhyme attests to the general satisfaction felt in connection with the first act of defecation of the day: 'Am besten ist der

CONTINUED...

Morgenschiss auch wenn er am Abend is(t).' [The best thing is the morning $%^&*, even if it is in the evening.]...The easy acceptance of such topics in daily life in contemporary Germany is signaled by an extensive four-part serial article 'Die Geschichte des Klo' [The History of the Water Closet]."

roasted beets
and carrots

This dish is a snapshot of autumn. Eat it or paint it. Actually, I shouldn't joke with my reading constituency. It's never good to skip a meal. It confuses your gut, and next thing you know, your regularity goes out the door. Eat this, and paint something else.

SERVES 4 AS A SIDE, COOL OR HOT

Preheat oven to 475°F. In a pretty casserole dish, toss the carrots and beets in 2 tablespoons oil, ½ teaspoon honey, ½ teaspoon salt, and pepper to your liking. Roast 25 minutes. Remove casserole from oven and toss in cleaned beet greens, stirring so they are distributed throughout and not floating on top. Add a bit more olive oil if things look dry. Add a dash of salt, too. Return casserole to oven for 5 minutes. Meanwhile, in a small bowl, whisk together the remaining honey and oil, shallots, vinegar, last dash of salt, and pepper, to taste.

When vegetables are dark in patches and beet greens look wilted and cooked, remove casserole from oven and toss with vinaigrette.

1 pound carrots, cut into
   ¼-inch slices
1 pound beets, peeled, halved,
   and cut into ¼-inch moons
Beet greens from above beets,
   chopped roughly
3 tablespoons olive oil
1 teaspoon honey, divided
½ teaspoon salt, plus 2 dashes
½ teaspoon pepper, or to taste
1 shallot, chopped
2 tablespoons balsamic vinegar
   (ideally white)

broccolini with bulgur and parmesan

1 cup medium-grind bulgur

1½ pounds broccoli rabe (or broccolini), stems trimmed

6 tablespoons olive oil

⅔ cup minced shallot

⅔ cup finely chopped walnuts

2 tablespoons lemon juice

1 cup grated Parmesan cheese, divided in half

Salt and pepper, to taste

Mark Bittman, the man who taught us *How to Cook Everything*, surely does write a lot of gut-friendly recipes. This one is off the charts. Seriously, a 10++ on the Go-Meter. Don't be frightened off by the intensely healthy sound of it. Your husband, kids, mother-in-law, principal, and babysitter—everyone—will love it. And if you leave a bowl of it in your fridge, it will mysteriously disappear...and the bathroom will be mysteriously locked for half the day.

SERVES 6 AS A SIDE

In medium bowl, combine the bulgur and 2½ cups boiled water. Set aside for 20 minutes, until bulgur is tender. Pour bulgur into a strainer set over a clean bowl. Reserve the soaking liquid. Set both aside. Cook the broccoli rabe or broccolini in boiling salted water (enough to cover), about 2 minutes; it will not be fully cooked. That's OK. Using tongs, transfer to a bowl of ice water and cool. Drain, then cut into 1-inch pieces and set aside. Place olive oil in large skillet over medium-high heat. Add shallots; sauté until soft, about 2 minutes. Add walnuts, and cook another 2 minutes. Add greens and bulgur, and dashes of salt and pepper. Cook another 3 minutes, stirring regularly. (If the

mixture looks dry, now's the time to add the reserved soaking liquid from the bulgar, by spoonfuls.) Stir in lemon juice; season with more salt and
pepper. Toss in half of the Parmesan cheese. The remaining Parmesan cheese should be placed on the
center of your table as an optional condiment.

BROCCOLI

Like other members of the cole crop (cabbage, cauliflower), broccoli is rich in balanced fiber—both soluble
and insoluble. It's been said that Thomas Jefferson, a man
with a green thumb, was one of the first Americans to
write about broccoli from a gardener's perspective, but
it took another hundred-plus years for the vegetable to
hit dinner plates in the States. That's when a couple of
intrepid Italians started to spread its gospel...

LEGUMES: PEAS, CANNELLINI BEANS, LIMA BEANS, NAVY BEANS, CASHEWS, AND PEANUTS

Many legumes share a consistently top o' the class nutritional profile: loads of fiber, protein, and minerals. Their high magnesium content is of particular interest, as magnesium in the diet correlates to a reduced risk for colon cancer. Nuts like cashews and peanuts are higher in fat than beans, but the Un-constipated Gourmet doesn't see that as a drawback. Finally, legumes are the blue-ribbon winners in a new fiber category called resistant starch. Resistant starch is science's shorthand way of saying "starch that's hard to digest." This hard-to-digest starch ends up raking the guts, stimulating good bacterial attacks, and producing fatty acids that fight cancer.

pea cakes

"Too basic. They won't amount to much." That's what you're thinking as you read through the ingredients here. Don't be fooled. These are more popular than mac 'n' cheese in my home, pair well with just about any meat, and, best of all, look like something out of Oz.

MAKES ABOUT 10 CAKES

Place peas, egg, onion, garlic, water, and oil into a food processor with a sharp blade. Purée. Add chickpea flour, baking powder, curry powder, and salt, and purée again. Batter should be smooth. In a large skillet, heat 2 tablespoons canola or olive oil. Using a ladle, make 3-inch pancakes. Bubbles will form when it's time to flip, about 3 minutes a side. The finished cakes will glow a lovely green beneath a brown crust.

1 cup frozen peas, thawed

1 large egg

1 onion, chopped roughly

1 large clove of garlic

2 tablespoons water

2 tablespoons olive oil

1 cup chickpea flour

1 teaspoon baking powder

1 teaspoon curry powder

1 teaspoon salt

2 tablespoons canola or olive oil

sweet pea purée

2 cups chicken broth

2 cups frozen or fresh sweet peas

¼ cup full-fat Greek yogurt

1 tablespoon chopped shallot

½ teaspoon salt

2 tablespoons snipped chives

1 baguette (optional)

This recipe took some fine-tuning, but my indispensable right arm, Rosanna, knew just what it needed—yogurt. And the addition of yogurt made it a 10 on the Go-Meter (without it, maybe a 7). Rosanna's culinary instincts are impeccable. She also lends a grassroots point of view to the project as a whole. I discovered this early in our relationship, when she emailed to say, "Somewhere back during those weight-obsessed college days, I ripped my guts out with a diet of prunes and peanut butter. Then I spent a semester in Hungary, where every meal that isn't cigarettes and espresso is prunes and pickles."

SERVES 4 AS A SIDE

Bring the chicken broth to a boil and add the sweet peas. Cook until just tender (3 minutes max, if frozen) and drain off broth, reserving. Cool both broth and peas to room temperature. Purée the peas and ¼ cup reserved broth, yogurt, shallot, and salt in the blender until smooth, adding more broth, if necessary, to make a soft, but not runny, purée. Serve, sprinkled with minced chives, on crostini (a toasted baguette with olive oil and salt) or use to prop up a lamb chop, pork chop, skirt steak, etc.

CULTURED YOGURT

Yogurt had its first revival back in 1910 when a Russian researcher claimed it was the key to Bulgarians' longevity. His research was probably overblown, but the digestive benefits of cultured yogurt are real enough to have spawned a thriving live-'n'-active yogurt industry a century later, complete with brand-name bacteria ("Bifidus regularis," "Bifidus digestivum"). But the news is older than both plastic cups and Russian researchers, and under humbler names, the very same bacteria have been chugging away behind the scenes for centuries.

How does it work? Certain healthful bacteria strains—*Streptococcus* and *Lactobacillus*—are added to milk and allowed to grow at a controlled warm temperature. Too much heat kills the friendly guys, as does long storage, leading to the "live and active" designation on carefully-handled commercial yogurt. Daily doses of live-culture yogurt populate the digestive tract with the friendly bacteria, which speed up digestive transit times in controlled studies.

CONTINUED...

Yogurt contains both curds (the chunky protein part) and whey (the translucent liquid that seeps out). People have known about the unconstipating effects of the lactic acid and probiotics in whey since the ancient Greeks. Galen (physician to five Roman emperors between 131 and 201 AD) enthused: "Whey...opens stoppings of the bowels; helps such as have the dropsy and are troubled with the stoppings of the spleen, rickets and hypochondriac melancholy..."

cauliflower with peas and ginger

I make this whenever I'm preparing Indian food. It's easy and tasty, and people who don't typically scarf cauliflower scarf this. The peas do most of the heavy lifting, but don't count out the cauliflower—it's no shrinking violet, fiber-wise.

SERVES 4 AS A SIDE

Place oil in a wide soup pot on high heat. Add cauliflower and ginger. Cover pot. Lower heat to medium, and cook 8 to 10 minutes, until cauliflower starts to brown. Stir once or twice. Add spices and peas. Cover again, stirring occasionally. Test a pea. When cooked through, serve. This goes very nicely with chicken tikka masala, Mango Chutney (page 45), and, if you dare, white Basmati rice and naan (known constipators!).

4 tablespoons olive oil or ghee

1 head cauliflower, cut into 1½-inch chunks

1 (1 inch) piece of ginger, peeled and minced

1 teaspoon salt

½ cup chopped cilantro

1 teaspoon turmeric

½ teaspoon garam masala

½ teaspoon crushed red pepper (or less, if you don't love heat)

1½ cups frozen green peas

soft, creamy polenta

4 cups water

Salt, to taste

1 cup medium-grain yellow
polenta (don't confuse this
with instant polenta)

4 tablespoons butter

1 cup cream cheese, room
temperature

Until recently, I've had nothing but trouble with polenta, from finding it in the stores (most stores only carry instant polenta, which cooks in minutes but feels like a mouthful of rubber) to cooking it. It would turn out too dry, too rubbery, or too bland. Then I stumbled upon this recipe at simplyrecipes.com—so basic, but so good. A slice of genius to add cream cheese. Sheer genius. And a perfect accompaniment to Fava Ragout (page 166), Tuscan Bean Soup (page 59), Lamb with Skordalia (page 145), Pulled Pork (page 154), or even Roasted Beets and Carrots (page 129).

SERVES 8 AS A SIDE

Boil salted water in medium saucepan. Pour in polenta, slowly—you want a light rain of polenta, not falling cats and dogs—whisking constantly until fully incorporated. Lower the heat to a simmer. Add butter. The polenta will look like bubbling lava as it thickens. Stir regularly for 30 minutes. It will start to pull away from the sides of the pot when it's ready. Right before serving, stir in the cream cheese, and salt to taste. You can continue cooking it past this point, but you must keep stirring to avoid scorching.

mujadarra

This is the Eastern Mediterranean version of beans and rice. Lentils replace the beans, and curry and fried onions add a sweet binder. This is just about the only place in the entire book where I have rice in a recipe. I debated its inclusion for a long, long time. But you simply can't make mujadarra without it, and the lentils more than offset the rice's presence. Note: The hotter the curry, the swifter the kick.

3 medium yellow onions, chopped

3 tablespoons olive oil

1 cup lentils

3½ cups water

1 tablespoon curry of your choice

2 teaspoons salt

1 cup long-grain rice

OPTIONAL TOPPINGS:

1 cup yogurt or crumbled goat cheese

1 cup chopped tomatoes

SERVES 4 AS A SIDE OR LIGHT MAIN COURSE

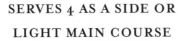

Fry onions in olive oil until nicely browned. Set aside. In a separate pot, cover lentils with water. Boil. Turn down to a simmer and cook 15 to 20 minutes. Add the onions, curry, and salt. Meanwhile, cook rice in another pot, following directions on package. When lentils are soft and rice is done, combine. Stir. Can (and probably should) be served with yogurt or crumbled goat cheese, and tomatoes.

sweet potato cakes

2 medium *sweet potatoes or*
   yams, peeled and shredded
   (about 4 cups)
⅓ cup *potato starch*
1½ teaspoons *salt*
1 teaspoon *pepper*
2 teaspoons *crushed garlic*
2 teaspoons *fresh thyme or sage,*
   chopped fine
⅔ cup *shredded onion or leek*
2 *eggs, lightly beaten*
2-3 tablespoons *canola or*
   corn oil

You must have a high mess threshold when making any kind of potato pancake—the splatter, the intense smell of grease—but, oh, how these babies go over with guests and guts. Serve with a thick Greek yogurt, sour cream, or ricotta cheese, or, if you're feeling zesty, Mango Chutney (page 45). A nice accompaniment to smoked meats, pork chops, and fish too.

MAKES ABOUT 20 PANCAKES

Preheat a parchment-lined cookie sheet in a 275°F oven. In a large bowl, combine sweet potatoes, potato starch, salt, pepper, garlic, and thyme or sage. Toss in the shredded onion. Pour in the beaten eggs, thoroughly coating the potatoes. If you think there isn't enough egg to hold together the pancakes (trust yourself), add another. Heat remaining oil in a large skillet on high heat. Cook 3 to 4 cakes at a time (about 4 inches in diameter and ¼ inch thick). Cook 4 to 5 minutes per side (cover them for the last few minutes). They should be nicely browned and cooked through. Place on the cookie sheet to keep warm while cooking remaining pancakes. Try to avoid stacking them on the cookie sheet (they'll get soggy).

SWEET POTATO

Popeye probably would've eaten sweet potatoes instead of spinach if he'd known about their extraordinary health properties. A common remedy for constipation in Asia, sweet potatoes are high in both fiber and potassium. Potassium strengthens the intestinal walls, among other moving parts. China is the sweet potato basket of the world, growing about 80 percent of the world's supply. Most of that supply was once eaten by humans, but now it's eaten by pigs—"regular" pigs.

entrees

An excerpt from "Der Wunsch" (The Wish), a German folk poem from early 1900, translated by folklorist and author, Alan Dundes.

"Nothing, oh friend, in this life can
Make us happy and content
Love, beauty, money, and honor
Excessive merriment in all areas;

Nothing may give us cheer

If the following is missing.

But if this one thing is lacking

Oh, then grieve and weep!

If you have to do without this,

You will die needlessly

This is the one thing on earth

That alone can make everyone healthy.

I wish you in all sincerity

Today at this very hour

This one thing, what should it be called?

Friend, it is the noble act of $%#^&*ing."

roast lamb with lima skordalia

Lima skordalia is a fancy name for "lima beans mashed with garlic and olive oil." It makes a terrifically tasty base for the lamb. And it's pretty. And you'll no longer think that lima beans are the legume with the self-esteem problem.

SERVES 6 TO 8

Marinate the lamb the evening before you plan to serve it. To make marinade, purée the yogurt, garlic, rosemary, lemon peel, pepper, and coriander in a blender. Rub this mixture over lamb, pushing into crevasses. Transfer to shallow dish. Cover and chill overnight.

You can prepare the skordalia a day ahead, too. Cook beans according to package directions and drain. Then cool slightly and purée in a blender with the garlic, oil, ½ teaspoon salt, and 2 tablespoons lemon juice. Taste. Add more lemon juice, salt, and pepper, as needed. Stir in parsley. Refrigerate, but bring back to room temperature for serving.

Prepare barbecue (medium-high heat) or preheat broiler. Season lamb generously with salt. Add pepper to your liking. For medium rare, grill lamb about 10 minutes per side. Remove to a platter and cover loosely with foil. Let stand five minutes. Place ⅓ cup skordalia on each dinner plate; lay several lamb slices on top.

¾ cup plain yogurt

6 large cloves garlic, chopped

1 tablespoon chopped fresh rosemary

1 teaspoon minced fresh lemon peel

2 teaspoons ground pepper

1 teaspoon ground coriander

1 (4-pound) leg of lamb, boned and butterflied

SKORDALIA:

1 (10-ounce) package frozen baby lima beans

3 large cloves garlic

¾ cup olive oil

½–1 teaspoon salt

Pepper, to taste

¼ cup lemon juice

2 tablespoons chopped fresh parsley

sauerkraut with apples and sausage

4 bratwursts (precooked),
whole or chopped into
1-inch pieces.

3 slices thick-cut bacon, cut
into 1-inch pieces

1 medium onion, peeled
and chopped

1 tablespoon butter

1 pound sauerkraut, drained

½ cup beef broth

2 tart apples, pared, cored,
and chopped

1 tablespoon brown sugar

1 bay leaf

¼ cup dry white wine

Salt and pepper, to taste
(you probably won't need it)

My husband grew up on a farm in Illinois and says there was nothing better than walking into the kitchen on a cold winter's day and inhaling his mom's sauerkraut with apples. To ensure that this recipe "works," make sure your sauerkraut is the real deal—i.e., no vinegar (which would kill off all the good bacteria), just salt, water, and time. Also, you may find two kinds of bratwurst at your local butcher, precooked and uncooked. I think the precooked works best for this recipe.

SERVES 4

In a large skillet, on high heat, sauté bacon until fat is rendered and bacon is crisp, about 7 minutes. Drain bacon on a paper towel and discard all but 2 spoonfuls of bacon fat. Deposit 1 spoonful of the remaining fat into another large skillet, and use the other spoonful in the original skillet. In the new skillet, sauté the onion in bacon fat and 1 tablespoon butter until tender. Add sauerkraut and sauté 1 minute. Add the broth, apples, sugar, bay leaf, and wine. Cook slowly on low heat, covered, for 10 minutes. Add bacon to sauerkraut. Continue cooking. Meanwhile, in original skillet, begin to sauté sausage on medium heat. Once the sausage is brown in places (about 10 minutes) and the sauerkraut has cooked 20 minutes, you have 2 options: you can add the sausage to the kraut now and cook the whole mix for another 10 minutes, or you can just cook the sauerkraut for another 10 minutes, pour it over the sausage, and serve. If you choose the latter course, keep the sausage on a low flame until ready to serve. Remove bay leaf from sauerkraut.

APPLES

The ancient fathers of nutrition and medicine, Galen and Hippocrates, prescribed sour apples for constipation. Their prescription still holds true. If you would rather not bite into an astringently tart apple, the sweet ones will do as well. Green apples—and to a lesser degree, all ripe apples—are especially high in natural pectin, a soluble fiber that nurtures the intestine.

falafel

1½ cups dried garbanzo beans

1 onion, peeled and quartered

4 cloves garlic, coarsely chopped

¼ cup fresh cilantro, oregano, or basil, coarsely chopped

2 tablespoons sesame seeds

2 tablespoons cumin

1–2 tablespoons Old Bay seasoning

1 tablespoon cayenne

1 tablespoon baking powder

¼–1 cup whole-wheat flour

Salt and pepper, to taste

Oil, for frying

I tried many, many, many falafel recipes before I found this winner. Most of the bad falafel recipes out there have too much spice and not enough crunch. A falafel ball should not overwhelm its surroundings (by surroundings, I mean the toppings that go with it— tzatziki, marinated onions, tahini sauce, etc.). This one is a perfect foil for the whole party. And every little ball is a 10 on the Go-Meter. Don't mess it up by pigging out on pita.

SERVES 6

Rinse beans and remove any brown ones. Cover with water and soak for at least 15 hours, until tender. Drain beans. Place them in a food processor with onion, garlic, and cilantro. Pulse everything to pulverize; stop short of a pasty consistency. Transfer to a bowl. Add spices, baking powder, and flour until the mixture is no longer wet and looks more like a coarse dough.

Heat about ½ inch of oil in a pan. Meanwhile, roll dough into 1½-inch balls, and then flatten them slightly. Set aside.

Once the oil has reached 350°F, fry falafel patties about 5 minutes per side, or until nicely browned (the oil temp should not exceed 375°F at any point; adjust flame to maintain temperature of oil). Drain on paper towels and serve with any or all of these toppings: Tzatziki (page 46), Tahini Dressing (page 93), onions marinated in good vinegar for 10 minutes, feta cheese, Hummus (page 53), or Baba Ganoush (page 49).

bean cakes/ veggie burgers

¾ cup chopped shallots

1 tablespoon olive oil

½ teaspoon salt

½ cup bulgur

1 cup water

1 cup canned, unsalted beans

   (black, chickpea, or pinto),

   drained and rinsed

¾ cup walnuts

2 garlic cloves, chopped

¼ cup chopped cilantro

¾ teaspoon cumin

¼ teaspoon cayenne

Salt and pepper, to taste

2 tablespoons olive oil,

   for frying

SAUCE:

½ teaspoon lime juice

½ cup cilantro

¼ cup mayo

Dash of salt

Serve it as a bean cake or a messy burger on a bun. Just serve it.

MAKES ABOUT 4 LARGE PATTIES OR 8 SMALL ONES

In a medium soup pot, cook ½ cup shallots in the olive oil until just limp. Add salt and stir. Immediately add bulgur and water. Bring to a boil, then simmer. Cook, covered, until water is absorbed, about 15 minutes. Remove from heat. Add beans. Purée ingredients in pot with an immersion blender. Add the walnuts, garlic, cilantro, cumin, remaining shallots, cayenne, salt, and pepper. Purée again. Cover pot and chill for 15 minutes. Meanwhile, prepare sauce by mixing lime juice, cilantro, mayo, and salt.

Remove bean mix from refrigerator. Heat a large skillet; when hot, add 1½ tablespoons olive oil. Don't bother making patties until this moment, because the mix is sticky and it's easiest to make patties at the very last moment (about 5 inches in diameter) and then drop them directly into the skillet. Salt them lightly after they're in the skillet (and again after you flip them). Cook about 4 minutes per side on medium heat. Serve as bean cakes or as veggie burgers. Either way, they're excellent with corn on the cob and coleslaw. Note: This will make a very loose burger that will ooze out of the sides of a bun, so if you have fussy eaters who prefer "neat" food, make them the cake version.

BULGUR

A Middle Eastern staple, bulgur is coarsely-ground sprouted wheat. Sprouted grains like bulgur have several advantages: they cook very quickly, their long-chain carbs are broken down into easily-digested simple sugars, and their vitamin content increases many times over.

STIFF UPPER LIP?

"In England, food which is traditionally thought to be 'good for you' always turns out to be a laxative. Thus, 'good for you' becomes an euphemism for 'makes you !@#$%.' The traditional British diet is highly constipating, you see—sausages, chips, and eggs. At the top of the 'good for you' list is tea, of course, with porridge and then green vegetables next and, I suppose, Heinz baked beans."

Granddaughter of a famous British historian who knows what she's talking about

pork pozole

Some call this soup, others, stew. Regardless of the designation, it's Latino comfort food. Hominy takes some getting used to—chewy, plump corn kernels?—but you will be rewarded for adapting to change. The hotter you make the pozole, the greater that reward.

SERVES 4

Using a spatula, make a spice rub by blending the salt, paprika, black pepper, coriander, dry mustard, and onion powder in a deep bowl. Add the pork cubes and coat with rub. Refrigerate at least 1 hour—ideally 5 or more. When the meat is ready, sauté the carrot and celery in olive oil in a large soup pot for 5 minutes on high heat. Add the hominy, including the juice from the can, spiced pork, salt, pepper, marjoram, chile en adobo, cumin, and onion. Add water if ingredients aren't covered with liquid. Bring to a boil. Turn down to a simmer. Stir every 10 minutes or so, until the pork is tenderized, for about 1 hour. Add liquid if the pozole shows signs of drying out. Stir in garlic right before serving. Adjust seasoning. Serve with cilantro and limes.

1 tablespoon salt

1 tablespoon paprika

1 tablespoon pepper

½ teaspoon coriander

½ teaspoon dry mustard

½ teaspoon onion powder

1 pound boneless pork shoulder (also called butt), cut into chunks

¾ cup chopped carrot

¾ cup chopped celery

1 tablespoon olive oil

4 cups (1 large can) hominy

½ teaspoon salt

½ teaspoon pepper

1 tablespoon fresh marjoram

1 minced chile en adobo

1 tablespoon ground cumin

1 onion, chopped

1 tablespoon minced garlic

1 cup chopped cilantro

6 lime wedges

pulled pork

¼ cup dark brown sugar

2 tablespoons salt

2 tablespoons paprika

1 tablespoon pepper

½ tablespoon ground coriander

½ teaspoon dry mustard

½ teaspoon cayenne pepper

½ teaspoon onion powder

3–4 pounds of boneless pork butt or shoulder

1½ cups apple juice

½ cup water

BBQ sauce (preferably one without corn syrup)

You're thinking, what could pulled pork possibly do for the gut? The answer is: not much. However, if you're eating meat, which I'm betting you are, and you're wondering, "Which meat is least sluggish?" consider this one. Why? Well, the long seasoning time, followed by the endless cooking time, do a good portion of the "breaking down" for you. And don't count out the spice factor. The gut responds to heat. Begin this dish 2 days before you intend to eat it (a Friday evening start is best, and then you can enjoy it as a Sunday dinner).

SERVES 6

Combine brown sugar, salt, paprika, pepper, coriander, mustard, cayenne, and onion to form a spice rub and smear over pork butt, coating every little bit of meat. Refrigerate overnight. The next morning, preheat your oven to 300°F. Sit pork butt on a roasting rack and sit rack inside a roasting pan. Pour apple juice and water into pan. The pork should not touch the juices (if it does, find a higher rack). Cover entire pan with foil. It should be a tight fit. Plan to roast the meat for about 5 hours. Then remove foil and cook another 30 minutes. The meat should be brown and falling apart when it's done. Transfer to a large glass baking dish. Cool for 20 minutes. When you no longer run the risk of burning your fingers, use 2 forks to break apart the meat. This meat gets better with age, so I recommend refrigerating it in a sealed container until the following day. Thirty minutes before you're ready to eat, preheat oven to 350°F and remove meat from refrigerator. Wait about 10 minutes. Place the meat in oven, uncovered, for 15 minutes. Serve with BBQ sauce and Polenta (page 138), Pea Cakes (page 133), or Sweet Potato Cakes (page 140). Or, if you're a die-hard BBQ person, buy a bun and serve as a sandwich, but you didn't hear that from me.

GUT EVANGELIST

As noted, one of the biggest names in constipation relief was John Harvey Kellogg, whose many tomes on gut health included *Colon Hygiene*, *The Crippled Colon*, and *The Itinerary of a Breakfast*. When in charge of the Battle Creek Sanitarium in the 1870s and '80s, he saw some 300,000 patients, most of whom he believed suffered from constipation. The seaweed derivative agar-agar and wheat bran were his favorite forms of fiber. From Kellogg we can trace the origins of bran muffins and all kinds of flaked dry cereals…and the evangelical hate of white bread.

James Whorton, Inner Hygiene

quick chorizo and chickpea stew

This is another adapted winner from Mark Bittman, author of *How to Cook Everything*. It's one of those dishes that looks like it must've taken hours to prepare. Not so.

1 tablespoon chopped garlic

¼ cup olive oil

1 (14-ounce) can chickpeas
   (including liquid)

¼ cup sherry

½ teaspoon salt

1 cup chopped chorizo sausage

½ cup chopped cilantro

SERVES 2

In a large skillet, sauté garlic in 1 tablespoon olive oil. After a minute, add drained chickpeas (reserve water from can for use in a moment). Sauté until chickpeas begin to brown, about 4 minutes. Then add chickpea liquid, sherry, and salt. Turn down heat and cook for 5 more minutes. Add chorizo (you can add more oil and sherry here, too, if the mix is looking dry). Simmer another 5 minutes. Garnish with cilantro. A green salad with creamy dressing pairs well.

mole

20 roasted almonds

¼ cup chopped banana, slightly
   unripe

2 corn tortillas

5 tablespoons soft butter

1 ounce soft semisweet chocolate

2 tablespoons chili powder (a
   good one will have cumin,
   salt, allspice, garlic, oregano,
   cloves, and coriander)

2 tablespoons sesame seeds

1 teaspoon cinnamon

1 teaspoon salt

1 tablespoon pine nuts

3 cups chicken stock

1 roasted chicken (about 4
   pounds)

ACCOMPANIMENTS:

1 cup Mango Chutney
   (page 45)

1 avocado, sliced

½ cup Cilantro Pesto
   (page 48)

8 Fresh Corn Tortillas
   (page 124)

There's an elaborate version of this that involves making your own chili powder and roasting your own chicken. If you buy a premium-quality chili powder and a preroasted chicken at a high-end market, you will end up with the same results as the cook who labored longer.

SERVES ABOUT 6

Purée the first 10 ingredients in a mixer with a steel blade, adding enough stock—about 1 cup—to create a smooth consistency. Store in refrigerator for a few days (for most flavor) or use right away by pouring contents into a soup pot, adding remaining chicken stock, and simmering for an hour. Pick meat off roasted chicken and add to sauce. Simmer 30 more minutes, at least.

Set accompaniments on your table. Serve the mole in soup bowls and direct guests to accessorize.

CHOCOLATE

"Good chocolate well made should agree with any stomach retaining the least digestive power," said Jean Anthelme Brillat-Savarin, the eighteenth-century French gourmand. Responsible for chocolate's lovely mood-lifting ability, theobromine is a powerful stimulant in proper concentrations (i.e., dark, *dark* chocolate). Like all stimulants, it speeds up the bowels. But what really shifts things to fifth gear is its high magnesium content, much like that old standby, milk of magnesia. Magnesium makes everything plump and comfy by relaxing intestinal walls and pumping water into the system. Brillat-Savarin became something of a chocolate evangelist. "When you have breakfasted well and amply, if you swallow a generous cup of good chocolate at the end of the meal, you will have digested the whole perfectly three hours later, and may then dine in comfort. Out of zeal for science, and by sheer force of eloquence, I have persuaded not a few ladies to make the experiment, although they thought to die of it; in every case they were delighted with the results, and none failed to glorify the Professor."

MORE ON MISO

Make sure you're buying "unpasteurized" miso if you're keen on getting ALL of its gastro benefits. Pasteurization is believed to wipe out the beneficial bacteria and enzymes that would otherwise colonize your gut and make everything down there one big, happy family. For the same reason, experts recommend that cooks avoid boiling miso (in soup, for instance), to avoid committing bacterial homicide. It's also noteworthy that miso's high salt content allows it to survive (happily) for months in your fridge; just be sure to keep it sealed and use very clean utensils to measure it out.

miso-marinated steak

This is just an excuse to eat filet mignon. But it's a good excuse, as the miso has that fermented thing that all the gut experts are hollerin' about.

SERVES 4

Mix the miso with chili paste and vermouth. Roll the steaks in the miso mix until completely coated. Refrigerate steaks for about 4 hours in a glass dish. Before grilling (or broiling), let steaks sit on counter for 10 minutes. Grill (close to flame) about 4 minutes per side, for medium-rare. Garnish with cilantro or parsley. I like to serve this with Sautéed Chard with Garlic (page 117) or Brussels Sprouts with Bacon and Shallots (page 118) and, of course, red wine (just to make sure the steak isn't clogging arteries while the fiber is clearing out everything else).

1 cup red miso

1 tablespoon chili paste

1 tablespoon dry vermouth

4 small filet mignons or 2 larger beef tenderloin steaks

½ cup chopped cilantro or parsley

chicken with prunes and mustard

16 pitted prunes

½ cup Madeira or Marsala wine (red wine works too)

1 chicken, cut up

1 tablespoon butter

1 tablespoon olive oil

1 sweet onion, sliced thin

½ cup grainy Dijon mustard

¾ cup chicken stock

¾ cup cream or crème fraîche

Salt and pepper, to taste

The recipe comes from a classy Seattle home chef who's a true maestro in the kitchen. Typically, she doesn't even use recipes—she just cooks by instinct. I'd heard amazing things about her chicken with prunes, so I convinced her to produce a recipe for lay cooks. Then I asked her daughter to test it for me. She did, and it tasted just the way she remembered. From a "regular" family in Seattle, to you. With love.

SERVES 4

Marinate the prunes in the Madeira or Marsala wine at least 3 hours, or overnight.

Dry the chicken pieces well and, using high heat, sauté in a large skillet in the butter-olive oil mixture. Brown on each side, using more butter-olive oil mixture if needed. Don't crowd the pan; do in batches, if necessary. Reserve on a plate.

On medium heat, sauté onion in remaining fat in skillet—or add a little more—until softened. Drain the prunes, retaining the wine. Now add that wine to the pan to deglaze. Add the mustard to pan and stir. Add the chicken stock, salt, and pepper and stir to mix. Put the chicken and prunes in pan. Cover. Cook gently, until pieces are done. The white meat will be done first, so remove when it is, and then remove dark meat. Start checking after 30 minutes. If any fat boils to the surface, skim off. When sauce has reduced some, add cream and simmer, stirring until thickened a little. Adjust seasoning. Return chicken to skillet to warm. Serve. Pairs nicely with whole-wheat couscous.

MORE POWERFUL THAN BIG OIL

At the Chicago World's Fair of 1893, there was a statue of a medieval knight on horseback made entirely of prunes. It was an ad, essentially, for California's latest big export, but it also spoke to the century's obsessions with the gut. "...Gastritis was listed as the third leading cause of death in the United States in 1900. Gastritis was a blanket term for most intestinal ills, but we need not trust the diagnosis to appreciate how seriously constipation was taken at the turn of the century."

Hillel Schwartz, Never Satisfied: A Cultural History of Diets, Fantasies, and Fat p. 131

fish tacos with corn salsa and fresh tortillas

½ cup Cilantro-lime-mayo
Sauce (from Bean Cakes/
Veggie Burgers, page 150)

1 cup Corn Salsa (page 54 or
store-bought)

1 cup shredded red cabbage

1 sliced avocado

1 can black beans

8 fresh corn tortillas
(page 124 or available at a
Mexican grocery)

1 pound flaky white fish
(tilapia, snapper, or trout)

1 teaspoon salt

Pepper, to taste

3 tablespoons flour

1 tablespoon olive oil

This sounds complicated, but it's really not—just lots of assembly and chopping. Make it with a friend, but go to the bathroom by yourself.

MAKES ABOUT 8 TACOS

Prepare Cilantro-lime-mayo Sauce, salsa (if you're not buying it), cabbage, and avocado, scoop them into ramekins, and arrange on your table. Get your beans going on the stove, and wrap your tortillas in foil and place in a 350°F oven to stay warm. Season fish with salt and pepper on both sides, and dredge in flour. Heat oil in a large skillet over high heat. Place fish carefully in oil, and fry until browned on both sides, about 3 minutes a side. Place hot fish on a serving platter and let guests assemble their own tacos with all the fixings.

seared scallop curry

This is a very simple dish, despite the length of the recipe. I've tried it with snapper and monkfish, and it works just as well.

SERVES 4

In medium saucepan, combine the water, bouillon cube, 1 tablespoon peanut oil, and salt. Bring to a boil. Add couscous. Stir twice. Remove from heat and cover. Let sit until tender, about 15 minutes.

Meanwhile, prepare scallops. Heat the remaining peanut oil in a large skillet over medium heat. Add ginger, garlic, and curry. Stir about 40 seconds. Add scallops. Cook 2 to 3 minutes per side, until flesh is no longer glassy and tops and bottoms are a nice brown. Add coconut milk. Scrape bottom of pan to remove sticky bits and cook for another 40 seconds. Remove from heat.

Mix 2 tablespoons cilantro and green onions into couscous. Place scoops of couscous in centers of four plates. Arrange a few scallops around these mounds, and pour sauce over. Garnish with cashews and cilantro. Place hot sauce on table as a condiment for those who like a little kick of spice.

¾ cup water

½ cube fish bouillon (without MSG)

2 tablespoons peanut oil

½ teaspoon salt

⅔ cup whole-wheat couscous

2 teaspoons minced ginger

2 tablespoons minced garlic

1 teaspoon mild curry powder

18 large scallops, rinsed, drained, and dried

1 cup coconut milk

2 tablespoons chopped fresh cilantro (plus 2 tablespoons for garnish)

½ cup chopped green onions

½ cup salted, dry roasted cashews, chopped

Thai hot sauce

fava ragout over polenta

Soft, Creamy Polenta
(page 138)

20 fava bean pods (or 1½ cups edamame)

2 tablespoons olive oil

½ teaspoon salt

½ cup chicken stock

1½ cups peas, freshly shelled or frozen

½ teaspoon lemon zest

¼ cup cream (or cream cheese)

4 ounces goat cheese

½ cup Parmesan cheese

Favas aren't available year round, so if you can't find them, substitute edamame, which works quite well, too. This makes a really lovely and easy dinner-party main course (for girls who eat light) or side (if you've got insistent meat eaters). Serve with Soft, Creamy Polenta (page 138). Lovely with a glass of cold white wine.

SERVES 2

Prepare the polenta first, according to the recipe. Fifteen minutes before the polenta is done, remove fava beans from pods. Bring 3 cups salted water to a boil in medium saucepan. Add fava beans to boiling water. Cook for 3 minutes on high. Drain, rinse with cold water, and squeeze inner green beans out of outer white husks. In medium skillet, heat 2 tablespoons oil, salt, and stock. When stock is bubbling, add peas. Cook until tender, about 2 minutes. Add favas. Stir in the lemon zest and cream (or cream cheese). Cook another minute.

In serving bowls, layer ingredients in this order: polenta, parmesan, ragout, and a final topping of goat and Parmesan cheeses.

"Sexual intercourse is bad for the stomach, especially if you have intercourse immediately of full stomach or while hungry..."

Marsilio Ficino, neo-Platonist, popular Renaissance physician, and philosopher and pal of the Medicis.

CHEESE

In his 1911 *Grocer's Encyclopedia*, Artemus Ward recommended the French habit of eating a little cheese for digestion with every meal, "especially when rich and old" (he was referring to the cheese). That said, cheese is a common scapegoat for constipation. However, like eggs, many people report anecdotally that cheese actually opens up their passages. Given the considerable variability of cheese—from the ubiquitous mild cheddar to moldy-veined, fungal, and leaf-packaged old gems—we advise you to discover your own anecdote.

ham and chard quiche

Quiche is all of God's greatest foods in a crusty bucket. So what if the crust here has nothing redeeming in it—at least where your slow guts are concerned—the filling makes up for it. The mercurial operator (eggs), plus the French standby (chard), plus the wheel-greaser (cheese), equals, "Pardon me, may I be excused?"

SERVES 6

Blend flour and salt on a cold surface or cutting board. Add butter and work into flour mixture with fingertips until dough resembles tapioca peas. Make a well in the center of the dough and pour in 2 to 3 tablespoons ice water. Still using your fingertips only, quickly blend water and dough. Add more water, if necessary, to get dough just barely sticky enough to hold together.

Touch it as little as possible (or you'll have chewy instead of flaky dough). Once it's in one piece, lay onto a sheet of plastic wrap, cover, pound into a disk, and refrigerate for at least 30 minutes. Once dough has chilled, preheat oven to 350°F. On a floured surface, roll out the dough ¼ inch thick. Try to roll it into a circular shape. Flip the disk over, so you know it's not sticking to anything and both

1 cup flour

½ teaspoon salt

6 tablespoons cold butter, cut into 10 pieces

3-5 tablespoons ice water

1 leek, white part only, chopped (or onion)

2 tablespoons olive oil

1 bunch Swiss chard, leaves and stems, washed and chopped

3 eggs

1½ cups half-and-half

½ cup Parmesan cheese

½ cup Gruyere cheese, shredded

Salt and pepper, to taste

½ cup finely chopped ham

sides are well floured. Place into a pie plate and flute edges (optional). When crust is in place, use a fork to prick the base in 3 or 4 places. Fit with parchment paper filled with pie weights or a sauté pan that sits neatly in the empty crust; precook the crust—with the weights—for 15 minutes. Set aside. Increase oven temperature to 375°F.

In a large skillet, sauté leeks in the olive oil for 2 minutes. Sprinkle with a dash of salt. Add chard and sauté until just wilted. Add another dash of salt. Toss ingredients. Remove from heat. Cool chard and leeks. Meanwhile, in a large bowl, beat eggs with half-and-half. Add the Parmesan and Gruyere cheeses, salt, and pepper. Add cooled chard mixture. Pour filling into pre-baked pie crust. Sprinkle ham over filling. Bake for 40 minutes; look for a browned top. Remove from oven. Let it sit for a few minutes before slicing, or the egg won't set.

desserts

"There are persons who complain of being unable to digest chocolate, and others who, going to the opposite extreme, declare that it contains too little nourishment, and passes too quickly through the system. It is most likely that the former have only themselves to blame, and that the chocolate which they are accustomed to...is of poor quality or badly prepared..."

Jean-Anthelme Brillat-Savarin, The Physiology of Taste, or, Meditations on Transcendental Gastronomy, 1825

brown rice pudding with figs

2 (13½-ounce) cans light
   coconut milk

3¼ cups whole milk

¾ cup short-grain brown rice

¼ teaspoon fine salt

½ cup sugar

1 cup chopped dried figs

½ cup sherry (optional)

Whipping cream

This is a time-intensive recipe, but the results are excellent. Make it on a day when you know you'll be home, puttering about, waiting to take care of business.

MAKES 4 TO 6 SERVINGS

Put the coconut milk, whole milk, rice, salt, and sugar in a small saucepan and bring to a boil over medium-high heat. Reduce the heat so the liquid simmers very gently. Cook uncovered. Stir occasionally, until rice is tender but chewy and absorbs most of the liquid, about 1½ hours.

Remove pudding from heat and transfer to a bowl, or divide among 4 to 6 individual bowls. Press plastic wrap directly on surface of pudding and cool in refrigerator, about 1 hour. While pudding is cooling, soak figs in sherry. Dress puddings with figs and whipping cream (whip it first, of course) before serving.

MY KINGDOM FOR A FIG

God bless Joan Fitzpatrick for her recent book, Food in Shakespeare; otherwise, I would never have found this quote in Henry V:

> Pistol: Die and be damned! And fico for thy friendship.
>
> Fleuellen: It is well
>
> Pistol: The fig of Spain
>
> Fluellen: Very good
>
> Pistol: I say the fig within thy bowels and thy dirty maw

Figs, a well-known purgative (a.k.a. laxative) even in Shakespeare's day, are here being wielded as an insult, i.e., the poop-maker of Spain.

prunes poached in red wine

10 black peppercorns

6 cloves

2 cinnamon sticks

2 whole allspice

2 (3-inch) strips orange peel

2 cups dry red wine, e.g.,

Navarre

¼ cup sugar

1 pound prunes with pits or

12 ounces pitted prunes

2 tablespoons triple sec

1 cup crème fraîche

This recipe appeared in the *New York Times* in March 2007. The author, Florence Fabricant, a perfectly lovely foodie, spends four paragraphs waxing romantic over her recipe's "earthy tannins" and the disarming blur of spice, sweet, and cream, but fails to mention the recipe's greatest attribute. If you make this for guests, perhaps let them guess which fruit they're tasting. I, for one, enjoy seeing the secretly thrilled expressions on their faces when I announce, "Prunes!" Florence suggests serving this dessert in stemmed goblets with whipped cream or crème fraîche. I agree. Pamper the prune, for once.

SERVES 4

Prepare the spice sachet first, placing all of the spices and peel into a sachet made from a 4x4-inch square of cheesecloth tied off with twine. Drop into a medium saucepan, and cover with wine. Bring to a simmer. Add sugar. Stir. Simmer another 10 minutes. Add prunes. Simmer 10 minutes more. Remove from heat. Add triple sec. Transfer brew to a metal bowl. Cover and set aside for 3 hours. Stir occasionally. Before serving, remove spice sachet. Serve at room temperature or cold, with crème fraîche.

WINE WITH HINT OF TAR, ANYONE?

"There are thousands whose habitual condition is one of languor and debility. Thousands suffering from Indigestion, Dyspepsia, and troubles of the Liver, Kidneys, and Bowels. What must they do? The system needs renovating and strengthening. New vigor must be infused in the digestive organs. The Stimulating, Regulating, Tonic properties of Dr. Crook's Wine of Tar will give a vigorous vitality to these organs. They must try it. They will soon feel its influence, and must persevere until the cure is complete. Keeping the Stomach and Bowels in a vigorous condition with Dr. Crook's Wine of Tar is the best defense against all diseases.

CONTINUED...

The rich medicinal qualities of Tar it contains would alone excite a regulating and strengthening action on the Stomach and Bowels, but there are Vegetable Ingredients of undoubted Tonic value combined with it, which cause it to build up the weak and debilitated, rapidly restore exhausted strength, cleanse the Stomach, relax the Liver, cause the food to digest, and make pure blood, removing Dyspepsia, Jaundice, Indigestion, and kindred complaints. Try one bottle. Ask for Dr. Crook's Wine of Tar."

Ad copy from the Presbyterian Cook Book, compiled by The Ladies of the First Presbyterian Church, Dayton, Ohio (Oliver Crook, Dayton, Ohio) 1873.

granola cookies

I feel like a charlatan while I'm making these cookies and a genius when I serve them. First rule: Make or buy oil-free granola with all the fixings (dried fruits and nuts of every shade). Second rule: Pay no attention to the mess spreading out on your cookie sheet...

1 (10-ounce) bag oil-free granola (or the same amount of your own, page 24)

½ cup butter, softened

½–¾ cup whole-wheat flour

MAKES APPROXIMATELY 30 COOKIES

Preheat oven to 375°F. Mix all ingredients. (Use more flour if the dough isn't holding together.) Place golf-ball size mounds on a cookie sheet (preferably a sheet with sides) about 1½ inches apart. Place sheet in oven and cook until tops of mounds darken. The cookies will fall and spread. Fear not. When the cookies look nice and golden, after about 12 minutes, remove from oven, and, while still hot, use a stiff spatula to remound each cookie. This is fun, sticky "work" (remember Rule #2: Pay no attention to the mess...). Don't expect perfection. Once the cookies are back in mounds, let them cool for about 15 more minutes. Pry them off the sheet and store flat on plates or in Tupperware (I don't advise stacking, unless you use wax paper to separate layers). Cook next batches in the same way.

rhubarb sauce

5 stalks rhubarb

½ cup sugar

½–1 cup water

¼ cup lemon juice

½ teaspoon lemon rind, grated

My Iowa buddy, Jennifer W., gave me this recipe along with one for sauerkraut, which her German in-laws swear by. Pour this sauce over just about anything, or eat solo, right out of a bowl (that's what I do).

MAKES ABOUT 4 HALF-CUP SERVINGS

Wash rhubarb well, and trim off and discard ends. Chop stalks into ½-inch pieces. Place sugar and rhubarb in saucepan with just enough water to keep mix from burning; cook until pieces are soft but not mushy, about 12 minutes. Add lemon juice and rind. Cook another 2 minutes. Serve warm or cold. Excellent with ice cream, almond cake, pancakes, or waffles.

RHUBARB

Some claim that the "rhu" in rhubarb comes from the Greek root word "rheo," which means "to flow." That would make bundles of sense, considering its purgative properties. My research turned up references to it in Chinese literature circa 2700 BC, when rhubarb was cultivated for medicinal purposes. It sounds like it was the Tylenol of its day, taken to fend off flu, plague, ancient STDs, and the like. You don't start hearing about it as a foodstuff until the Italians get a hold of it in the seventeenth century. Then rhubarb tarts and pies started appearing in bakeries, and the good times rolled...or flowed.

almond cake
with booze

1½ cups almond flour

1 cup whole-wheat cake flour

1½ teaspoons baking powder

½ heaping teaspoon salt

10 tablespoons unsalted butter

⅔ cup plus 1 tablespoon sugar

7 ounces almond paste

1½ teaspoons vanilla extract

3 large whole eggs

3 large eggs, separated

SYRUP:

1¼ cups cream sherry or
    Grand Marnier

2 tablespoons sugar

2 tablespoons butter

½ cup lemon juice

½ teaspoon lemon peel

This is best prepared in the morning, so the booze has a chance to soak and flavor the cake by the time dessert rolls around that evening.

SERVES 8

Preheat oven to 325°F. Butter and flour a 10-inch round or square cake pan. Blend dry ingredients in medium bowl. Using electric mixer, beat the butter and ⅓ cup sugar until whipped. Beat in almond paste. Add vanilla. Add 3 whole eggs. Beat until blended. Add 3 egg yolks and blend. Stir in dry ingredients. In separate bowl, beat 3 egg whites until soft peaks form (this is good exercise and may also get you moving). Add remaining 1 tablespoon of sugar to whites. Continue beating until just stiff. Gently fold whites into main batter with rubber spatula. Pour batter into greased cake pan.

Bake about 45 minutes, until set. Cool cake in pan, about 1 hour. Meanwhile, prepare booze syrup. Combine the booze, sugar, and butter in a small saucepan. Stir over low heat until sugar dissolves. Simmer about 15 minutes. Remove from heat. Add lemon juice and peel.

After an hour of cooling, pierce about 20 holes in cake with a toothpick or tine. With a spatula, spread half of syrup over cake. Let sit for another hour. Flip cake onto pretty serving platter. Pierce holes in bottom of cake. Brush remaining syrup over cake. Let cake stand 30 more minutes. Cake may be slightly messy from the flipping and piercing, so serve with a lovely "mask," like fresh whipped cream, rhubarb sauce, or a dusting of powdered sugar.

ALMONDS

Almonds are a girl's best friend. That's the refrain among the pregnant women in my circle. When it seems no food will make it down past the bun-in-the-oven, almonds manage to go the distance. There are lots of reasons why, according to almond lobbyists. Reason #1 is: the almond's massive calcium, magnesium, and potassium content. Reason #2 is: the laxative properties of almond oil. While almonds can be found in several recipes in this book, health purists say they're best blanched and eaten by themselves as an after-dinner snack.

fruit crisp three ways

½ cup sugar

2 tablespoons lemon juice

1 tablespoon cornstarch

1 cup oats

½ cup brown sugar

½ cup flour

½ teaspoon salt

⅓ cup butter, softened

vanilla ice cream

BLACKBERRY-APRICOT
CRISP:

10 apricots, pits removed, sliced
　into quarters (or 4 peaches,
　sliced into eighths)

2 cups clean blackberries

APPLE-RHUBARB CRISP:

4-5 apples, cored and sliced
　into eighths (if you want more
　fiber, keep skins on; if you want
　a mushier crisp, remove skin)

1½ cups rhubarb, chopped into
　half-inch pieces

BLUEBERRY-MANGO
CRISP:

3 cups roughly sliced mango

3 cups blueberries

Giving three versions of fruit crisp allows you to make it with just about any fruit you've got on hand. There are myriad permutations of possibilities, so feel free to mix and match. The key is pairing fruits with equivalent cooking times. Even with the butter, there isn't a gastroenterologist who'd snub this dessert.

SERVES 6

Preheat oven to 375°F. Lightly butter a glass baking dish (13×9 inches, or thereabouts). Combine the sugar, lemon juice, corn starch, and fruits in bowl. Mix well. Pour into the baking dish.

In medium bowl, combine the oats, brown sugar, flour, and salt. Add butter. Stir with a fork until mixture is crumbly. Sprinkle over the fruit. It should cover every bit of the fruit; if it doesn't, make more topping. Bake until browned and bubbly, 30 to 40 minutes. Serve warm, with vanilla ice cream.

FRUIT FOCUSED

"There is a prevailing notion that the free use of fruits, especially in summer, excites derangement of the digestive organs. When such derangement occurs, it is far more likely to have been occasioned by the way in which the fruit was eaten than by the fruit itself. Perhaps it was taken as a surfeit dish at the end of a meal. It may have been eaten in combination with rich, oily foods, pastry, strong coffee, and other indigestible viands, which, in themselves, often excite an attack of indigestion. Possibly it was partaken of between meals, or late at night, with ice cream and other confections, or it was swallowed without sufficient mastication. Certainly, it is not marvelous that stomach and bowel disorders do result under such circumstances. The innocent fruit,

CONTINUED...

like many other good things, being found in 'bad company,' is blamed accordingly. An excess of any food at meals or between meals is likely to prove injurious, and fruits present no exception to this rule. Fruit taken at seasonable times and in suitable quantities, alone or in combination with proper foods, gives us one of the most agreeable and healthful articles of diet. Fruit, fats, and meats do not affiliate, and they are liable to create a disturbance whenever taken together."

Ella Eaton Kellogg (nurse, author, dietitian, and wife to Dr. John Harvey Kellogg, famous for his Battle Creek-based health regimen and his high fiber cereal, later to become the Corn Flakes we know and love when his brother got his hands on it and added sugar), Science in the Kitchen. A Scientific Treatise on Food Substances and their Dietetic Properties, Together with a Practical Explanation of the Principles of Healthful Cookery, and a Large Number of Original, Palatable, and Wholesome Recipes, 1893

pomegranate tapioca pudding

This is another autumn-only dish. I've tried it with other fruits, but there's something about the pomegranate—besides its special digestive properties—that makes it uniquely suited for this tapioca. Plus, it looks coy.

¼ cup small pearl tapioca

2 cups coconut milk

1 pomegranate

2 egg yolks

¼ cup sugar

Mint

SERVES 6

Place the tapioca and coconut milk into a saucepan and let soak for 40 minutes. Meanwhile, extract seeds and juice from pomegranate by cutting it open over a bowl and picking out seeds. Discard hull. Set aside seeds and juice. When tapioca is done soaking, mix in egg yolks and sugar. Cook over low heat for 10 minutes; to avoid boiling and scorching, stir often. Tapioca should be cooked through (tapioca beads should be soft, not chewy). Fold in the pomegranate seeds and juice. Refrigerate for 1½ hours, or overnight. Serve in wine glasses with sprigs of mint.

sweet potato pie

1 pound *sweet potatoes, each
    cut into 3 big chunks*

1 cup *flour*

½ teaspoon *salt*

6 tablespoons *cold butter, cut
    into 10 pieces*

3–5 tablespoons *ice water*

½ cup *butter, softened*

⅓ cup *granulated sugar*

⅓ cup *brown sugar*

¼ cup *milk*

¼ cup *cream*

2 *eggs*

½ teaspoon *ground nutmeg*

½ teaspoon *ground cinnamon*

1 teaspoon *vanilla extract*

Whipped cream

This pie has a magic effect on pregnant women. They say they only want a small piece, and then they're asking for thirds. Perhaps it's the look of the pie— i.e., misshapen and unpolished, an ugly ducking compared to its more popular cousin, the pumpkin pie. Pregnant women, feeling the first pangs of maternal instinct, take it under their wings...if they only knew what the pie was giving them in return.

SERVES 8

First, boil or bake sweet potatoes in skins (at 400°F) for 40 to 50 minutes or until soft. While potatoes are cooking, prepare crust. Blend the flour and salt on a cold surface or cutting board. Add butter. Work into flour mixture with your fingertips until the dough resembles tapioca peas. Make a well in the center of the dough. Pour in 2 to 3 tablespoons water. Still using your fingertips, quickly blend the water and dough. Add more water, if necessary, to make the dough just barely sticky enough to hold together. You want to touch it as little as possible. Once it is in one piece, lay it onto a sheet of plastic wrap. Cover. Pound into a disk. Refrigerate for at least half an hour.

While crust is in the refrigerator, remove skin from sweet potatoes. In electric mixer, blend the potatoes, butter, and sugars. Add the milk, cream, eggs, nutmeg, cinnamon, and vanilla. Beat until the mixture is smooth.

Preheat oven to 400°F. On a floured surface, roll out dough to ¼ inch thick. Try to roll it into a circular shape. (It's not easy, but try.) Flip the disk over so you know it's not sticking to anything, and both sides are well floured. Press into a pie plate. Flute edges (optional). Pour filling into unbaked pie crust.

Bake at 350°F for about 1 hour. The pie will puff up a little and possibly form a slit down the middle when done. Serve with fresh whipped cream.

peanut butter cookies

½ cup butter

½ cup sugar

½ cup brown sugar

1 egg

1 teaspoon vanilla

½ cup peanut butter

1¼ cups whole-wheat flour

½ cup flax seed meal, millet flour, or whole toasted millet

1 teaspoon baking soda

¼ teaspoon salt

Okay, here's the truth—these are peanut butter cookies with a little somethin' added to make them your best bowel friend. If I told you in the title that the special ingredient was flax seed or millet, you might be scared to eat these cookies—scared they'd taste like something you tried in the 1970s that you're still purging from your guts. Trust me: you can't taste the special ingredients here. They're like guardian angels who hide in the shadows and take care of business. Note that there are three grain options for this recipe—in addition to whole-wheat flour, you may make the cookies with flax seed meal, millet flour, or whole toasted millet; or, do as I do, and divide the dough into thirds (before adding the flax or millet flour or toasted millet) and try it three ways. Each style looks slightly different, which makes for a pretty contrast on a display plate.

MAKES 2 DOZEN

Preheat oven to 375°F. Grease a cookie sheet. Whip the butter and sugars in an electric mixer. Add the egg and vanilla. Combine thoroughly. Add peanut butter. Mix well. Add the flour, flax seed meal (or millet flour or toasted millet*), baking soda, and salt. Drop by large spoonfuls onto a baking sheet and bake for 10 minutes or until golden.

*To toast millet, just place the grains in a small sauté pan. Heat on a medium flame, until just starting to brown. Shake the pan often. Cook for 5 to 7 minutes.

FLAX SEEDS

Flax has certainly had its share of the health limelight lately. Famous for its omega-3 fatty acids, it's just as useful for its high fiber content. Flax fibers swell very nicely in water, creating soft bulk. They also contain lignans, a form of soluble fiber that promotes the growth of healthy gut bacteria and has been suspected of curing most ills known to humankind. Unlike some fiber-rich seeds that, when added to gourmet food, transform it into something akin to dirt, flax actually makes many foods taste a bit better because of its oily consistency, which comes in particularly handy for vegetarians who use it to replace eggs in baked goods.

chocolate beet cake

3 large red beets, quartered

2 cups water

½ pound butter

8 ounces unsweetened chocolate

4 eggs

2 cups sugar

1½ cups flour

2 teaspoons baking powder

½ teaspoon salt

1 pint heavy whipping cream

Mint

Another winner from my extraordinary assistant, Rosanna. This mixes the power of two key foods—chocolate and beets—to produce a memorable shade of cake.

SERVES 10

Cover beets halfway with water. Add a dash of salt. Boil until beets are tender. Drain and let cool. Remove skins and purée (you may have to add a bit of water to get smooth). Set aside.

On medium heat, melt the butter and chocolate. Don't let them boil. While letting this mix cool a little, preheat oven to 350°F and grease two 9-inch round cake pans. Line bottoms with parchment paper. Flour the sides. Set aside.

Pour the chocolate mixture into a mixer and beat with the eggs and sugar. In another bowl, whisk together the flour, baking powder, and salt. Gradually fold the dry mix into the chocolate mix, alternating with beet purée.

Pour the batter into baking pans and smooth tops. Bake until risen in center and an inserted toothpick comes out clean, about 40 minutes. Cool 5 minutes in pans. Remove cakes from pans. Cool completely on rack. Meanwhile, in chilled bowl, whip cream until thick enough to spread as an icing. When cakes are cool, stack with a layer of whipped cream in between. When serving, add another dollop of whipped cream and a sprig of mint to each slice.

flourless chocolate cake with raspberries

8 ounces semisweet chocolate, coarsely chopped

4 ounces bittersweet chocolate, coarsely chopped

1⅓ cups plus 2 tablespoons sugar

¾ cup boiling water

1½ cup unsalted butter, softened

6 large eggs

1 tablespoon instant espresso powder (or a warm shot of espresso)

1 tablespoon vanilla extract

1 cup raspberries

Powdered sugar (optional)

It's best to make this cake in the morning so it has all day to set. Four hours is the minimum set time, but six is ideal.

SERVES 6

Preheat oven to 350°F. Butter all sides of a 9-inch springform pan. Line bottom of pan with a round of parchment paper (buttered on both sides).

Using a mixer with a metal blade (or a blender), mix chocolates and 1⅓ cups sugar. Pour boiling water over chocolate mixture. Process for 10 to 15 seconds, until the chocolate is completely melted. Add butter. Blend until combined. Add the eggs, espresso, and vanilla and process until mixture is smooth, a few seconds. Scrape sides of bowl and blend a few more seconds. Pour batter into springform, and smooth top.

Place the pan on a baking sheet and bake for about an hour. Edges will puff up. Center of cake should be set (i.e., when you touch the center, it should not be liquid). Cool cake on a wire rack for 35 minutes. Cover and refrigerate 4 hours or longer.

While cooling, wash raspberries and sprinkle with remaining sugar. Serve cake slices with berries, or if you prefer unadulterated chocolate, just decorate top with powdered sugar.

RASPBERRIES, BLACKBERRIES, BOYSENBERRIES, CRANBERRIES

Berries offer a high fiber-to-calorie ratio. A cup of raspberries, for instance, contains 8 grams of fiber, but only 60 calories. Many berries, like blueberries and cranberries, are naturally high in pectin, a form of soluble fiber that nourishes intestinal tract bacteria. Boysenberry juice is a mild laxative.

PERSIMMONS

"There is a saying in the persimmon country that per-simmons are 'good for dogs, hogs, and 'possums.' This, however, is declared to be a gross injustice to a very valuable product." So said *The American Health Journal* in 1916. The problem, then and now—people don't know what to do with persimmons. Most have one bad experience eating an unripe one, get an astringent mouthful, and never go back. Mistake. There are two basic varieties: soft persimmons (e.g., hachiya) and crisp persimmons (e.g., fuyu). According to traditional Chinese medicine, soft persimmons regulate chi and break up stoppages in the bowel. But, according to others, all persimmons are good; they contain twice as much dietary fiber as apples. And if you eat the peel, I can almost guarantee results.

persimmon pudding

My amazing assistant, Rosanna, invented this pudding and posted it to her blog, Paprikahead.com. She then offered it to me as an excellent example of what the persimmon can do when put to the test. Her original description is so lovely, I'm sharing it here: "Think 'pudding' as in 'bread pudding'…what seems mere cake at first slice turns all syrupy-spicy-custardy under a generous lather of cream and then disappears to leave you dazed and dreamy-eyed… Having nearly a quart of persimmon on hand, I reduced the milk and splashed in all my silky red-orange pulp with wantonly intemperate glee. A certain prodigality was due if we were to forget the threat of barbarian invasion (winter strawberries) for one gloriously debauched night of persimmon indulgence. Incidentally, the sun never sets on the persimmon empire, since persimmons are native to all four hemispheres."

6 tablespoons butter

3½ cups hachiya persimmon pulp

¼ cup cream

½ cup whole milk

2 tablespoons honey

3 tablespoons maple syrup

½ teaspoon vanilla

3 eggs

1½ cups flour

¾ teaspoon baking powder

¾ teaspoon baking soda

½ cup brown sugar

1½ teaspoons cinnamon

½ teaspoon ground nutmeg

1 teaspoon salt

⅔ cup crushed walnuts

⅓ cup golden raisins

1½ cups heavy cream, for whipped cream

SERVES 8

Preheat the oven to 325°F. Grease a large springform pan. Set aside.

Melt butter. Let it cool for about 5 minutes. Set aside. Mix together the persimmon pulp, cream, milk, honey, maple syrup, vanilla, and eggs.

In another bowl, mix together the flour, baking powder, baking soda, brown sugar, cinnamon, nutmeg, and salt. Add wet ingredients to dry and combine well. Set aside. Lightly brown walnuts in a dry skillet over low heat. Cool. Add to batter, along with raisins and the slightly-cooled butter. Pour batter into pan and slide it into oven, with a baking sheet underneath to catch any drips. Bake 45 minutes. "The pudding should rise in the center and form deep glassy rifts while still quivering in invitation," Rosanna says. "Serve with pillows of whipped cream."

almond-lemon macaroons

This is an adaptation of a recipe that ran in the *New York Times*. It's perfect for gluten-intolerant observant Jews during Passover, and pregnant women any time.

4 cups roasted almonds (reserve about 30 for decoration)

2 cups sugar

2 eggs

Zest of 2 lemons

MAKES ABOUT 24 COOKIES

In a food processor fitted with a steel blade, blend the almonds (minus the 30 reserved for garnish), 1½ cups sugar, eggs, and zest. Pulse until a dough that holds together forms. Cover processor bowl or transfer to a covered bowl and refrigerate overnight.

Preheat oven to 350°F. Line baking sheet with parchment paper. Place remaining sugar in a bowl. Pinch off pieces of dough and roll into 1½-inch rounds. Dip into sugar and coat on all sides. Press a whole almond into each cookie. Place 1 inch apart on cookie sheet. Bake for about 10 minutes; they'll turn slightly golden but remain soft. Cool completely. Store in an airtight container.

REMARKABLE FRUIT

"...I heard a certain Protos, an orator and fellow-citizen, say that his bowels are evacuated after eating harsh pears and apples...Following his bath, he drank a little water, then took fenugreek and radishes, and those things that many people eat before tasting anything else. Subsequently, having drunk a moderate amount of sweet wine, he ate mallows with oil and fish sauce with a little wine, and following this, fish, pork, and poultry. Then when he had had one, maybe two drinks, after a short interval he ate harsh pears. Then, when we had been for a stroll, after he had walked about a little, his bowel evacuated in a remarkable fashion."

Galen, physician to the gladiators and Marcus Aurelius, On the Properties of Foodstuffs

pear tarte tatin

What needs to be said about tarte tatin? It's the prima ballerina of the tart world. Often made with apples, I think it moves better with pears.

SERVES 8

To prepare the crust, pour flour onto a slab of marble or a clean counter. Sprinkle in salt and mix with your fingers. Cut cold butter into flour. Incorporate by pinching with fingertips only. When the dough is the consistency of poppy seeds, make a well in the center and pour in half of the ice water. Still using just your fingertips, bring the driest flour in contact with water. Touch dough as little as possible. Add more water, if necessary. Stop when entire ball of dough just holds together. Wrap dough in plastic. Flatten into a disk. Refrigerate for 1 hour.

Place pear slices in a bowl with the lemon juice. Set aside.

Preheat oven to 425°F. In an ovenproof skillet, heat 1 cup sugar and ¼ cup water until bubbly and beginning to brown/caramelize. As soon as sugar begins to brown, turn off heat. Remove skillet from burner. Beware of hot sugar—you don't want it to touch your skin. Carefully lay pears into hot sugar, making a pretty fan design. Sprinkle with remaining ¼ cup sugar and chopped butter.

1 cup flour

1 teaspoon salt

6 tablespoons cold butter, cut into small pieces

3–4 tablespoons ice water

6 firm pears, peeled, cored, and cut into thin slices

Juice of 1 lemon

1¼ cups sugar

¼ cup water

5 tablespoons unsalted butter, chopped into about 6 pieces

Vanilla ice cream

Roll out dough on a floured work surface into a 10-inch round about ¼-inch thick. Place dough on top of pears. Press edges down between pears and inside of skillet. Poke a few holes in the top crust with a fork. Bake for about 45 minutes, or until pastry is golden brown and the juice bubbling up the sides is syrupy and sticks to the back of a wooden spoon.

Carefully remove skillet from oven. Let it sit 5 minutes. Then, using oven mitts, hold a large plate firmly over the pan, and invert both plate and skillet quickly and carefully, in one seamless motion. Serve warm, with vanilla ice cream.

THE UN-CONSTIPATED GOURMET

poached ruby
pears with caramel

Here's a red vixen of a dessert made just from fruit. Pears: naughty and nice.

SERVES 8

Peel, halve, and core the pears. Combine the sugar, water, port, beet, lemon peel, and vanilla in a soup pot. Bring to a boil. Simmer for 10 minutes. Add pears. Simmer until cooked through, 10 to 15 minutes. Test with a skewer (it should go through the pear easily, but you don't want the pear too soft). Drain on a rack. Chill. Save 1 cup of the poaching liquid to make caramel.

For caramel, place 1 cup poaching liquid in a small saucepan. Simmer until reduced by half, about 10 minutes. Add cream and cook until sauce turns a golden color and coats the back of a spoon.

Serve pears in bowls with warm or cold caramel sauce (and ice cream, if you want extra decadence). Pears can be made a day ahead and chilled (separate from the poaching liquid). Make the caramel the day you need it.

4 pears, not too soft, not too hard

1 cup sugar

1½ cups water

½ cup Port wine

1 red beet, peeled and quartered

1 (2-inch slice) lemon peel

1 tablespoon vanilla

1 cup heavy cream

Ice cream (optional)

mexican wedding cookies

1 cup walnuts, toasted in
sauté pan

1½ cups whole-wheat
pastry flour

1 cup oat flour

½ teaspoon salt

1 cup unsalted butter

½ cup sugar

Splash vanilla extract

Splash bourbon (optional)

¼ cup powdered sugar,
for dusting

This is a great recipe from the online collection at 101Cookbooks.com by whole-grain cook extraordinaire Heidi Swanson. Her cookbook, *Super Natural Cooking*, is one of my favorites, and gorgeous to boot. This is her spin on Mexican Wedding Cookies. I told her it was just perfect for the book, and she let me include it here.

MAKES ABOUT 18 COOKIES

Purée nuts in a food processor until they form a fine meal (don't make into buttery lump by processing too long).

In a medium bowl, mix dry ingredients (minus powdered sugar). Set aside. In an electric mixer, beat the butter and sugar until creamy. Add the vanilla and bourbon (optional), and then the nut meal. Slowly add the mix of dry ingredients, blending until a stiff dough forms. Move dough to a square of plastic wrap. Tear off another square of equal size and place atop the mound. Pound the mound into a disk that's about ½ inch thick (that's how thick you'll want your cookies to be, so don't ignore this direction like I did the first time I made them). Cover on all sides with wrap and place in freezer for 10 to 15 minutes. Preheat oven to 325°F. Use a 1-inch round cookie cutter (or a shot glass if you're without a formal cookie cutter) to press out neat circular cookies. Place them on a baking sheet lined with wax or parchment paper. They don't need to be more than an inch apart, as they don't spread much. Bake for 12 to 15 minutes, or until bottoms of cookies begin to brown. Remove from oven. Don't move or touch them until they're totally cool (they're very fragile while hot and will fall apart if messed with). When completely cool, dust with powdered sugar.

bourbon truffles

8 ounces dark chocolate (70 percent cocoa butter), divided in half

4 ounces butter

3 tablespoons bourbon

You could keep a bowl of these right outside the bathroom if that weren't incredibly tacky.

MAKES ABOUT 20

To prepare filling, bring 1 inch of water to a simmer in a shallow saucepan. In a small metal bowl, place 4 ounces chopped chocolate and butter. Set the bowl in hot water. Stir occasionally until melted. Remove from heat. Whisk in bourbon, a little at a time, until smooth and shiny. Set entire mix in freezer to cool. Stir every 10 minutes, until firm enough to shape into balls. Make 1-inch balls. Place on a tray. Return to freezer to set completely.

To prepare outer coating, chop remaining chocolate into gravelly chunks. Place half in the little bowl used above and use the same technique (setting it in the hot water) to melt. Add reserved chunks and remove from heat. Stir until they, too, have melted. Remove truffle tray from freezer and prepare to roll the truffles in warm chocolate coating. Working slowly, take 1 prepared truffle and roll it in melted chocolate, until coated. Scoop it up with a fork and gently tap the fork on the side of the pan so the excess chocolate drips off and falls through the tines. Scoot wet truffle into a receptacle you can refreeze.

When all truffles are dipped, return to the freezer to set for about 20 minutes. If you're going to eat them right away, they can sit on the counter in a cool room; if you're going to eat them within a few days, store in refrigerator; if you're going to eat them next month, freeze. Always bring to room temperature when serving so insides are properly soft.

ALCOHOL

Booze speeds up intestinal activity. It's a recognized phenomenon, but nobody's quite sure how it works. Here's one theory: stress causes constipation, and alcohol reduces stress. Take care, though—alcohol also dehydrates the body. Constipating dehydration is much less mysterious than alcohol in its effect on the bowels.

special elixirs

"Whortleberries, commonly called huckleberries, dried, are a useful medicine for children. Made into tea and sweetened with molasses, they are very beneficial, when the system is in a restricted state, and the digestive powers out of order."

Lydia Maria Francis Child, The Frugal Housewife, Dedicated to Those Who Are Not Ashamed of Economy, 1830

Dr. Bart Kummer, the esteemed New York City gastroenterologist I told you about at the beginning of this book, is a water pusher. In his 25 years of experience, almost no ingredient has done more to help his constipated patients. "Water is cheap, nontoxic, and doesn't require a prescription. I can't recommend it enough."

This short chapter is about water and its potent stepchildren—coffee, tea, and booze. Perhaps because they are so easy to toss back and so quick to take effect, they represent a particularly controversial subset of the un-constipating family. My research often turned up hilariously contrary advice:

"Milk in small quantities has for many a constipating effect; taken in large quantities it often has a laxative effect, because of the amount of water with which the system is deluged; in other cases, existing constipation is intensified by this practice..."

Anna Lindlahr and Henry Lindlahr, M.D., The Lindlahr Vegetarian Cook Book and ABC of Natural Dietetics, 1918.

The Lindlahrs write like they're trying to avoid a lawsuit.

Starbucks doesn't advertise the relationship between a venti cappuccino and the gut, but if you've ever waited in line outside a Starbucks bathroom, perhaps you put two and two together. In England, tea time is practically a national pastime devoted to baiting the bowel. In India, tea is similarly applied; in addition to the ubiquitous chai, whose caffeine can't help but roil the gut, many Indian families rely on a simple blend of hot water with lemon called "nimbu pani," (nimbu means lemon and pani means water). The nimbu pani combination can be varied and embellished; sometimes sugar, salt, lime, and even pepper are added so it can be salty and sweet at the same time. Though it's prepared hot, it's served cold. And word on the street is, it regulates the whole body, not just the digestive tract—which can only be a good thing.

Booze falls into a slightly different category. That category would be poison. The body will do all kinds of back-flips to get poison out (hence the whisky s$$ts).

What's worth noting here is that a goodly amount of liquid (preferably *not* the poisonous variety) is sometimes all you need to solve your seemingly insurmountable problem. In the following pages, I've shared a few special drinks that you can whip up at home, the sort that add a little spice to life or at least to plain H_2O.

ginger water

½ cup ginger, peeled and chopped into large chunks

6 cups water

¼ cup honey

¼ cup lemon juice (to be added when tea is served)

M.F.K. Fisher, in her 1961 book, *A Cordiall Water: A Garland of Odd and Old Receipts to Assuage the Ills of Man & Beast*, devotes all of Chapter 11 to purges, laxatives, and diuretics, most of them in the form of drink. She tells the story of an actress who performed a seasonal three-day "cleanse" to cure a "bitter yellowish feeling in her liver." M.F.K.'s mom called this cleanse a "good course of the sprouts" or a "tail-raiser." The cleansing concoction involved castor oil and olive oil, taken "with teas and more stimulating cordials made from many pleasant-tasting herbs." "Pleasant" must've meant something different back then.

Now, ginger water IS actually pleasant and a nice twist on plain water, while milder than tea or coffee. It can be kept in the refrigerator for up to a week in a sealed container.

MAKES 6 GLASSES

In a large saucepan, bring the ginger chunks and water to a boil. Lower to a simmer and cover for 30 minutes. Stir in honey. Remove from heat and cool. Transfer to a sealable container and store in the refrigerator. When ready to serve, reheat or serve cold. Add lemon juice.

HOT WATER

Folk medicine, Ayurvedic teachings, Mrs. Beeton (the Fanny Farmer of Britain), and medieval health guides all tout the cleansing properties of a draft of hot water. Nobody's sure exactly why it works, but warmth is nothing more than molecular movement. And movement…there's no harm in downing a dozen ounces in the middle of the day and giving it a try.

chai

2 tablespoons ginger, cut into
   thin rounds
2 cinnamon sticks
2 teaspoons black peppercorns
   (less, if you don't like it
   too spicy)
10 whole cloves
6 cardamom pods
6 cups cold water
6 bags of black tea
   (preferably Darjeeling)
Whole milk, for blending
¼–½ cup (packed) golden
   brown sugar (or less, depending
   on your sweet tooth)

If you've been looking for an alternative to the over-sweetened, chalky chai available in the beverage aisle of your local grocery store, here's a recipe for you. It's an excuse for a tea party on a rainy day. Beware: The caffeine sensitive will be bouncing off the walls.

SERVES 6

Throw the first 5 ingredients into a medium saucepan. Using a potato masher, lightly crush or bruise spices. For milder tea, add 6 cups water now and bring to a boil over high heat. Reduce heat to medium-low. Partially cover pan. Simmer gently for 10 minutes. Remove from heat. Add tea bags and steep 5 minutes. Discard tea bags. Add 2 cups whole milk and ¼ to ½ cup sugar. Bring the tea to a simmer over medium heat, whisking until sugar dissolves. Strain the chai into a teapot and serve hot. For stronger tea, add 1½ cups water to the crushed spices. Cook on high heat about 10 minutes, until water reduces; keep a close eye. Turn off heat. This is now a base that you can store in the fridge and use to make individual servings. To make 1 serving, in a small pot, boil 1 cup water with 1 tablespoon (or more) of spice mix for about 5 minutes.

Remove from heat. Add 1 tea bag and steep for 5 minutes. Discard tea bag, and add 1 cup of whole milk and 1 tablespoon sugar (or more, if you like it sweeter). Return to heat and simmer until sugar dissolves, about 5 minutes. Strain. Serve hot.

TEA

"If you have a heaviness and foulness of stomach, and… you are more costive than usual, drink plentifully of green tea, till all the slime be got off your stomach," says William Ellis in the 1750 *Country Housewife's Family Companion*. Rich in antioxidants, the caffeine in tea stimulates the nervous system much like coffee. Tea, however, also contains many tannins, which are purported to have a constipating effect. Taking care not to oversteep the tea prevents it from being too tannic.

chili hot chocolate

1⅔ cups milk

½ vanilla bean, split lengthwise

1 red chili pepper, split, with
seeds removed

1 cinnamon stick

1½ ounces bittersweet
chocolate, grated

Doctors have been prescribing chocolate as a digestive aid since chocolate's been around. This is chocolate laced with a bit of spice to double its efficacy.

SERVES 2

In medium saucepan, on low heat, warm milk with the vanilla bean, chili pepper, and cinnamon stick. After about 2 minutes, whisk in grated chocolate. Continue to simmer until melted. Remove from heat. Cover and let flavors meld, about 10 minutes. Strain out spices and serve. (It may need to be reheated. Just don't boil it.)

mulled wine

Your doctor won't recommend this. And I'm not suggesting you turn it into a weekly mainstay. However, when winter comes along and you find yourself cooped up in the house with a jug of wine, cinnamon sticks, and a brick in your belly, no one would chastise you for concocting the brew.

SERVES 8

Pour wine into a soup pot. Add spices. Cook over low heat, about 5 minutes. Add sugar. Stir until dissolved. Add brandy. Heat thoroughly, but do not allow to boil. Add lemon and orange. Continue to cook, 1 hour, over lowest heat. Taste occasionally and add more sugar if you prefer it sweeter. Serve hot.

4 quarts dry red wine
(zinfandel, merlot,
burgundy, etc.)

1 cup sugar

6 cinnamon sticks

12 cloves, whole

⅛ teaspoon allspice

⅛ teaspoon mace

1½ cups brandy

1 lemon, sliced

2 oranges, sliced

"My very dear cousin, before I write to you, I must go to the closet. Well, that's over. Ah! At least I feel lighter, a weight is off my heart; and now I can guzzle again…"

A line from a letter Mozart wrote to his cousin in 1777, translated in *Life Is Like a Chicken Coop Ladder: A Study of German National Character Through Folklore*, by the late Alan Dundes.

emergency
recipes!

According to Vagbhata (one of the three classic writers of Ayurveda, which is the most ancient of the six recognized Indian systems of medicine), irregularity is often caused by the weather. Some of Vagbhata's culinary cures for the rainy season (or the Time of Taking) include the following: matured grains, spiced broths, dry-terrain game meat, soups, aged wine and liqueur, sour cream with dark salt, dusted with mixed spiced water…But if it is a really bad weather day, one's food should be obviously sour, salty, and oily, as well as very lean, light, and mixed with honey. One should avoid the following: river water, buttered barley water, sleeping during the day, and sunshine.

Paraphrased from The Roots of Ayurveda: Selections from Sanskrit Medical Writings, *translated by* Dominik Wujastyk.

This is a short and potentially dangerous chapter. You'd better have a true emergency if you're reading these pages; otherwise, turn back. This is not food to trifle with. Any one of the four concoctions below (I don't think they deserve to be called recipes) will almost certainly do a number on your insides. (An alternative name for this chapter might be "Inside-Out.") These all work best with chasers of warm water (at least 8 ounces). Find a cozy spot in the house to read or nap afterward. Certainly, don't leave the house for at least 3 hours after dining.

three ounces of dark chocolate

This is the only emergency "procedure" that can be used on the run, and I still prefer you try it at home. But if you find yourself in a bind at work or while traveling, here's your cure. I like to keep a bar of dark chocolate (at least 65 percent cocoa butter) on me at all times, for those "just-in-case" situations. It gives me a sense of safety. Again, chase with warm water or coffee, if you dare. And for Pete's sake, splurge on quality chocolate; there should be more chocolate than sugar in the bar.

COFFEE

A European physician visiting the Turks and Arabs in 1582 found them drinking a beverage "black as ink and helpful against stomach complaints." Not much later, Europeans recognized coffee's marvelous stimulating properties, in addition to its digestive effects, and collectively sobered up when they traded morning beer for morning coffee. Just like when you get "scared $hitless," caffeine stimulates production of adrenaline, which raises blood sugar and sets off the digestive machinery. The end result is peristalsis, the series of squeezes that moves roughage along. Essentially, caffeine tricks the body into thinking it's been nourished, and the gullible intestines hurry to make room for new food. Undeniably effective in the short term, some critics believe it creates dependence and increases constipation in the long run.

bran muffin with hot, milky coffee

Prepare the Enlightened Bran Muffins on page 5. Have your milky coffee nearby. (Use low-fat, whole milk, or half-and-half. You're not doing your stomach any service by feeding it acid without proper amounts of fat, too.) Slowly eat the muffin. Between bites, take sips of hot, milky coffee. This should not be eaten while running for the bus or train in the morning. It should not be eaten during a meeting at work. Miss the first hour of work if you must. Just sit still and wait for action.

prunes with warm brandy

Buy a package of good, unsulfured prunes. Place 5 prunes on a plate. (I don't recommend more than 5, tempting as it is to go for the gusto.) Set aside. Put a kettle of water on the stove. Heat just until it starts to whistle. Pour this hot water into a medium pot and immerse your preferred drinking glass (a snifter is ideal, but don't sweat it if you don't have one) in the water. Leave it to sit for a few minutes while you work on a crossword puzzle. After five minutes or so, pour a shot or two of brandy into your warmed glass. Warm the brandy further by holding the glass in your warm hand for a few minutes. Sit. Kick your feet up. Nibble slowly on the prunes, chewing each one completely. Chase each prune with a sip of brandy. This is not a process to rush, as the food will likely hit your system like a steamroller. Follow this "meal" with a cup (or more) of warm water. This is best tried after dinner.

DRIED FRUITS

I've tried to avoid competition between these recipes and ingredients, but with dried fruit, it's hard not to separate the men from the boys. Figs, apricots, and dates pack the most fiber (in a field crowded by old timers and newcomers like blueberries, prunes, tart cherries, figs, apples, pears, raisins, bananas, papaya, pineapple, and peaches). In fact, one fig has more fiber than two apricots, so if you're counting calories... Blueberries claim the highest antioxidants, which are associated with protection against disease and the effects of aging. One word of warning: If you're going to load up on dried fruit, do yourself a favor and drink lots of water too, otherwise you're going to find yourself with a dry mouth and a brick in your gut that refuses to pass.

CONTINUED...

A special note on prunes, the undisputed old maids of constipation for the past 100 years. Artemus Ward, author of the 1911 *Grocer's Encyclopedia*, speaks for us all when he defends the shriveled old girl: "No fruit can boast higher food value than prunes, for they contain large amounts of both protein and easily digestible sugar. They are also valuable as a laxative and the water in which they are stewed is for this reason frequently employed as a vehicle for purgative medicines. It seems a pity that cheap humor and poor jokes should be laid so heavily on such excellent, serviceable fruit, which is always good, always in season, and capable of use in a great diversity of ways…" Ditto, ditto, ditto.

galette
double-dose

Double the Galette recipe on page 2. Serve with warm maple syrup or warm Rhubarb Sauce (page 178). After eating, drink an 8-ounce glass of warm water. Sit. Kick your feet up. Wait. It's a good breakfast cure if you wake up sluggish and have no place to be.

RICE BRAN

Known as "nuka" in Japan, rice bran is often pickled or used to wash dishes. Why not use its high fiber content to wash your guts? Friendly intestinal bacteria tend to prefer rice bran, as it contains a good balance of soluble and insoluble fiber. Rice bran is appearing in more baked goods, particularly those for gluten-intolerant eaters.

TEN ADDITIONAL EMERGENCY PROCEDURES

If you're terribly impatient, have been pacing in front of the loo for too many days to count, and need a few nongourmet ways to kick-start your engines, consider these activities. Like my recipes, they're a mix of lore and conventional wisdom…and magic.

1. Go for a long walk (at least an hour) at high speed; then lie down for an hour

2. Plan not to leave the house for the first two hours after walking

3. Spend 10 minutes on your back, bringing legs to your chest, one at a time, like you're cycling

4. Sit on your feet for 20 minutes

5. Drink 4 ounces of water every hour for 8 hours

6. Get warm, if you're chilled

7. Relax your gut, and breathe into it (if you have a habit of sucking it in, quit it)

8. Chew gum for half an hour

9. Bake something that makes the house smell great

10. Don't age

*Those of you tempted to smoke a cigarette when constipated would not be alone when falling back on this emergency procedure. Nicotine, like chocolate and caffeine, gets things moving. More than a billion people on the planet fall back on this method of maintaining regularity. However, this is the same billion that will be competing with you for a lung transplant in your golden years. Not recommended.

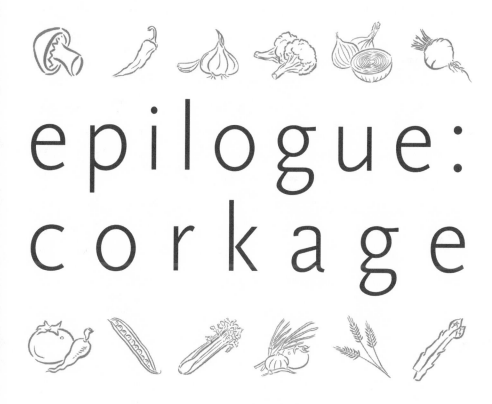

epilogue: corkage

"To stop looseness of the bowel, boil a sheet of writing paper (rags) in 3 pints of milk, serve with sugar."

William Ellis, The Country Housewife's Family Companion, 1750

A friend made the very wise assessment that if I was going to write a whole book about how to get the guts "moving," then I'd better have a few recipes at the end that teach folks how to slow the gut down. I decided to heed this advice. The following are some failsafe remedies for what's commonly known as Montezuma's Revenge. They are not elaborate in the same sense as their predecessors, because when faced with the opposite of a corked gut, you simply want to create a bulky, starchy dam. The fancier or more complicated the dam, the less likely it is to work. If it ends up that you've got something clinically wrong—like giardia, God forbid—then nothing you eat or drink is going to help you until you get on prescribed medication. Once you're stabilized, return to this section of the book and begin eating again. And please accept my condolences.

baked potato with olive oil and salt

SERVES 1

Take 1 baked potato and drive a food nail through it. Turn the oven to 425°F (this can be made in a toaster oven, as well). Sprinkle salt on skin (which you can eat if you want, but be warned that it's got fiber in it, and fiber is not what you need right now). Bake the potato on a cookie sheet for 45 minutes to an hour. Don't worry if the skin gets brown. Slice open, avoiding steam burns. Sprinkle more salt, drizzle olive oil, and eat. Avoid doctoring with dairy—cheese or butter. However, feel free to go crazy with the salt.

pile of toast

Use your instincts.

milk toast

SERVES 1

Take 1 slice white or wheat bread, preferably stale, and toast it until light brown. Place warm toast in 1 cup warm, low-fat milk. Let milk soak into toast for 2 minutes. Eat like cereal—i.e., with a spoon. This dish is complemented nicely with nothing. My friend Catherine swears by its reliability. When desperate, try anything.

white rice

Please. Follow directions on the bag.

matzo pancakes

SERVES 2

Of these options, this is probably the most palatable, but beware—for some strange reason, matzo behaves as a laxative for some people. If you're certain you're not one of those, onward: take 3 matzos and break into small pieces. Place in a bowl and cover with warm water for several hours or overnight. Drain soaked matzo in a strainer and press out as much water as you can with a large spoon. Separate 2 eggs. Beat the whites until stiff. Add the lightly beaten yolks to the matzo, along with dashes of salt and cinnamon. Fold in egg whites. Heat a large skillet. Add butter. Ladle several 4-ounce portions into the pan. Cook slowly until browned on 1 side, about 4 minutes. Turn over and cook another 4 minutes. Serve with a good sprinkle of cinnamon and sugar, or sour cream and jam. These are exceptionally light and fluffy matzo pancakes.

French Dressing and a Sponge Bath...

"Many persons seem totally ignorant of what causes and prolongs constipation. The mind has a more powerful influence over this than over any other disease; for this reason impress upon the patient that the given course of diet is curative. Among the numerous conditions which cause and prolong this disease are the overeating of starches and the drinking of tea and coffee with sugar and cream with meals…Too concentrated food, and too great a variety at a meal. Drinking too little water between meals. Softened bread of toast by dipping in tea or coffee. Overeating of sweets, stewed dried fruits with sugar. Eating heavy meals early in the morning, whether hungry or not. Disobeying the call of nature until a more convenient hour. Stewed fruits with meals or at the end of a meal as a dessert, are nine out of ten times constipating. The few 'don'ts' that follow may help you in selecting a suitable diet: Don't eat an early breakfast, especially in bed. Don't eat fruits stewed with sugar at the end of meals. Don't drink at the beginning of a meal. Don't preface your dinner with a soup. Don't each rich sauces. Don't eat mayonnaise on vegetables; use French dressing. Things To Do. Bathe or sponge every morning; rub until the skin is aglow. Drink immediately a glass of cool, not iced, water. In thirty minutes drink a cup of clear coffee. If hungry a little later, eat fruit, or a soft-boiled egg and bacon. Drink a pint of cool, not iced, water between breakfast and luncheon. Masticate every mouthful of food thoroughly. Drink at the end of the meal. Buttermilk and brown bread make an exceedingly good luncheon or supper. Take fruits with cereals, vegetables with meat. At bedtime eat four or five tablespoons of scraped turnip, or grated carrot or apple, or two ounces of peanut brittle, or a half-pint of freshly-popped corn. When ready for bed, drink a glass of cool, not iced, water."

Sarah Tyson Rorer (author of *The Philadelphia Cook Book*, *Mrs. Rorer's New Cook Book*, and many other valuable works on cookery), *Mrs. Rorer's Diet for the Sick*, 1914.

I particularly love this random assortment of techniques for fending off constipation, written by the woman many consider America's first dietician. It's nearly a hundred years old, but there's something about it—perhaps the cocksuredness—that captures the present, too. Read any newspaper tomorrow morning with your bran muffin and you will probably find a scientific discovery that upends everything we previously believed about health and sets us on a newly styled course of self-preservation. The recipes in this book represent my best attempt to share the gamut of constipation "cures" whirling around the universe today. But who knows what tomorrow brings...

Contact

If you'd like to contribute a recipe, visit www.theunconstipatedgourmet.com. There you can read more about the process of making *The Un-Constipated Gourmet*, you can talk to other readers, and you can email me your secret recipes (which I'll test in my kitchen and post if tasty *and* effective).

Bibliography

Not a complete record of resources, by any means, but a solid representation of the substance and range. Many of the older works are available—in full—online.

Beeton, Isabella. *The Book of Household Management Comprising Information for the Mistress, Housekeeper, Cook, Kitchen-Maid, Butler, Footman, Coachman, Valet, Upper and Under House-Maids, Lady's-Maid, Maid-of-all-Work, Laundry-Maid, Nurse and Nurse-Maid, Monthly Wet and Sick Nurses, etc. etc.—also Sanitary, Medical, & Legal Memoranda: with a History of the Origin, Properties, and Uses of all Things Connected with Home Life and Comfort.* Britain: (Publisher unknown), 1861.

Beecher, Catherine, and Harriet Beecher Stowe. *The American Woman's Home.* London: Rutgers University Press, 2002.

Brillat-Savarin, Jean-Anthelme. *The Physiology of Taste, or, Meditations on Transcendental Gastronomy,* tr. by Anne Drayton. New York: Penguin Classics, 1994.

A Book of Fruits & Flowers, 1653, ed. by C. Anne Wilson. London: Prospect Books, 1984.

Burr, Hattie A. *The Woman Suffrage Cook Book, Containing Thoroughly Tested and Reliable Recipes* for Cooking, Directions for the Care of the Sick, and Practical Suggestions, Contributed Especially for this Work. Boston: Hattie Burr, 1886.

Child, Lydia Maria Francis. The Frugal Housewife, Dedicated to Those Who Are Not Ashamed of Economy. Boston: Carter and Hendee, 1830.

Collins, Anna Maria. The Great Western Cook Book, or Table Receipts, Adapted to Western House-wifery. New York: A. S. Barnes & Company, 1857.

Davidson, Alan. The Oxford Companion to Food, first ed. New York, Oxford University Press, 1999.

Fisher, M.F.K., A Cordiall Water: A Garland of Odd and Old Receipts to Assuage the Ills of Man & Beast. New York: North Point Press, 1961.

French, Edwin Charles. Food for the Sick and How to Prepare It: With a Chapter on Food for the Baby. Morton, Louisville: John P. Morton & Company, 1900.

Gerard, John. A Catalogue of Plants Cultivated in the Garden of John Gerard, in the Years 1596-1599: Edited with Notes, References to Gerard's Herball, the Addition of Modern Names, and a Life of the Author, ed. by Benjamin Daydon Jackson. London: (Published by priv. printer), 1876. Original from Oxford University.

Hale, S.J. The Good Housekeeper, or, The Way to Live Well and to Be Well While We Live, Containing Directions for Choosing and Preparing Food in Regard to Health, Economy, and Taste. Boston: Weeks, Jordan, & Company, 1839.

Katz, Sandor. Wild Fermentation: The Flavor, Nutrition, and Craft of Live-Culture Foods. Vermont: Chelsea Green Publishing Company, 2003.

Kelder, Peter. Ancient Secret of the Fountain of Youth. Gig Harbor: Harbor Press, 1998.

Kellogg, Ella Eaton. Science in the Kitchen. Chicago: Modern Medicine Publishing Company, 1892.

Markham, Gervase. The English Housewife, ed. by Michael R. Best. Montreal: Queen's University Press, 1994.

Milham, Mary Ella. Platina: On Right Pleasure and Good Health. Tempe, AZ: Medieval & Renaissance Texts and Studies, 1998.

Miller, Daphne. The Jungle Effect. New York: Harper Collins, 2008.

Montefiore, Judith Cohen. The Jewish Manual Practical Information In Jewish And Modern

Cookery with a Collection of Valuable Recipes & Hints Relating to the Toilette. London: (Publisher unknown), 1846.

Presbyterian Cook Book, Compiled by The Ladies Of The First Presbyterian Church. Dayton, Ohio: Oliver Crook, 1873.

The Roots of Ayurveda: Selections from Sanskrit Medical Writings, tr. by Dominik Wujastyk. New York: Penguin Classics, 2003.

Schivelbusch, Wolfgang. Tastes of Paradise: A Social History of Spices, Stimulants, and Intoxicants. New York: Vintage Books, 1992.

Schwartz, Hillel. Never Satisfied. London: The Free Press, 1986.

Vehling, J.D. Apicius, Cookery and Dining in Imperial Rome, c. 100 B.C. to 300 A.D. pp. 46-47.

Ward, Artemus. The Grocer's Encyclopedia: A Compendium of Useful Information Concerning Foods of All Kinds. How They are Raised, Prepared and Marketed. How to Care for Them in the Store and Home. How Best to Use and Enjoy Them —And Other Valuable Information for Grocers and General Storekeepers. New York: Stationers' Hall, 1911.

Whorton, James. Inner Hygiene. New York: Oxford University Press, 2000.

Acknowledgments

The agent, Victoria Skurnick, who, after sitting next to me for one week and listening to my idle chatter, decided I was someone with an important culinary message. The editor, Hillel Black, for his keen eye, and his diplomacy on all matters. The rest of the Sourcebooks team, Carrie Gellin, Jennifer Crosby, and Anne Hartman, in particular. The unembarrassed family: Mom, Dad, Kyle, Charlotte, Eric, Dagmara, Ephraim, and the supportive clan in Illinois. The employers, Levine Greenberg Literary, for their enduring faith in a West Coast loon. The heavy-lifters, Rosanna Nafziger, whose only payment was the recipes she tested; and Andrea, who cared for Charlotte while I typed. The instigators, Arielle Eckstut and David Sterry, for getting me into this business. The constant boosters: Renanah and Gina, for thinking about guts with me through the years; Carla, for saying she'd pay to be involved; Anika, Kate, and Meredith, for egging me on; and Luba, Jeanne, Nicole, and Delia, for always chuckling. The coffee-break squad, Tracy and everyone at Cover to Cover Bookstore who rolled their eyes—their unique style of support. The artist, Emily Stackhouse, for giving a "face" to the Un-constipated Gourmet. The other indispensable members of the volunteer squad: Ken Albala, Anya

Binsacca, Lesley Bonnet, Anne Bramley, Georgeanne Brennan, Catherine Byrne, Lynne Carstarphen, Marilyn Cohan, Barby Cohen, Lori Cohen, Chris Colin, Allison Eshel, Asha Fridland, Leonie Gombrich, Andrea Hirsch, Sandor Katz, Julie Jares, Bart Kummer, Stephen Jaffe, Michael Lukas, Kirsten Main, Daphne Miller, Suzanne Morrison, John Polizzi, Joan Prime, Andy Raskin, Joshua Room, Michael Skrzypek, Karen Solomon, Amy Standen, Heidi Swanson, Marianne Tanzer, Monika Verma, Jennifer Wagner, Tara Austen Weaver, Leah Wolchok, James Whorton, Lynne at foodtimeline.org, and Cindy at 1000eggs.com. The pros: Anish Seth, for his amazing contributions to the scatological world (*What's Your Poo Telling You?*) as well as his foreword (a gastroenterologist's perspective), and my friend, Frances Largeman-Roth, who graciously volunteered to write the second foreword (a nutritionist's perspective) while bogged down with her own cookbook (xv). And the saints who got me through that rough patch: Christine, Lelia, and Shay. A debt of gratitude to all. I am such a lucky, lucky girl.

Index